TELL
Everyone
ABOUT
Jesus

A MEMOIR OF FORGIVENESS

To Father Kowalczyk,
May God richly bless the
Our Lady of the Sacred
Heart Church for
bringing me to Jesus.
Donna M Joseph
October 25, 2023

TELL
Everyone
ABOUT
Jesus

A MEMOIR OF FORGIVENESS

Donna Marie Joseph

Vincent Publishing Company, Inc.
Knoxville, Tennessee USA

Published by the Vincent Publishing Company, Inc.
Knoxville Tennessee USA

First Printing May 2023
ISBN 978-1-949220-01-8 (Paperback)
ISBN: 978-1-949220-02-5 (eBook)

FOR DADDY

Who once said to me, "Oh! Can you imagine if together we could come up with a way to tell the whole world about Jesus? Wouldn't that be fun? Oh, how I would love to do that with you someday!"

Joseph James Busshart
Mar 7, 1931–Feb 18, 2002

Thank you, Daddy. The greatest way we can tell others about Jesus is through the story of how you first told me.

FOR MAMA

Who taught me where God was and how to talk to him when I was three. I went to the kitchen one day to ask Mama who this "God" was that I kept hearing about. While handing me a cool lemonade, through the grandeur of her explanations, she planted an everlasting thirst for God in my heart.

Patricia Frances Busshart
Feb 19, 1933–Sept 3, 2018

A beaming smile spread across Mama's face as she stretched her arms out to show that God was the biggest one of all, the one who made the whole world. God made the sun and the moon and the stars and the sky, the beaches and the parks, the trees and the flowers, all the people, all the animals, and all the bugs. He even made *Santa Claus*. God is bigger than she or Daddy, and he can do *anything*.

The more Mama spoke about this great God, the more questions I had and the more I wanted to see him. I could not understand why my siblings were not begging to go see this wonderful God—all the time.

I asked Mama where God lives.

"He lives in a beautiful place called 'heaven,' in the clouds."

God must be a lot like Santa Claus then, I figured, living in an enchanted place in the sky. Like Santa, he must have some magical way to get into people's houses—even undercover.

"Where is God, right now?" I asked.

Mama waved her hand in the air with a gesture that conjured magic. "Right now? God is *everywhere!*" So, I went off to look for God—everywhere in the house.

After a thorough search, I asked my next older sister, Brenda, where God was and she answered, "At the church." So, I went and got our Sunday coats and brought them to Brenda. "Let's go to the church. I want to see God."

"No, Donna, he's not like that! He's not the *man* at the church. Nobody can see God, and I don't know where he is—Oh! Go ask Mama! She's the one who started all of this!"

I went back to Mama in the kitchen. "I looked under all the beds, in all the closets, in the bathroom cabinet, behind the couch and all the curtains, but I can't find God anywhere in the house. Is he... *hiding?*"

"Uh—no, God's not hiding."

I ran my hand across the kitchen wall. "Is he... in the *walls?*"

"Well, no, he's not like that."

I whispered in her ear. "Is he being *sneaky?*"

"Uh—no, God's not sneaky."

Then Mama sat me on the cupboard and explained where God is, so I could forever understand. She pointed to my heart and said, "You can't see God because he's inside you. And he stays *right there, in your heart,* all the time. That way, he makes it real easy for you to talk to him whenever you want. That's what 'praying' is—just talking to God inside your heart. So go lie under the willow tree, look up to heaven, and talk to God. And I *promise* you, *promise* you," she said firmly, pointing her finger at me, *"God will hear your every word, every time."*

Thank you, Mama, for the best life lesson you ever taught me. God does always listen. Listening, God loves.

CONTENTS

PART I

THE
SPIRITUAL
JOURNEY

CHAPTER 1

INTRODUCTION

> Your word is a lamp to my feet and a light to my
> path.
> —Ps 119:105

AT A SOCIAL GATHERING around a campfire, a young woman shared her thoughts: "Our family just moved to this area from out of state, and suddenly I find myself soul searching. I'm a stay-at-home mom, a supportive wife, and now a new member of a community. I understand these are important roles for my relationships with others, but I want to know who is the 'I' in all this, and why am I here?"

The young woman realizes her roles in relationships with others are significant, but in themselves, they are not equivalent to the *actualized I* within her. We are more than our roles: parent, spouse, community member, or one of a particular profession. We must first discover who we are in relation to ourselves before understanding the purpose of our other relationships.

Tell Everyone About Jesus: A Memoir of Forgiveness (Part I) entitled "The Spiritual Journey" includes a collection of metaphysical articles based on the Holy Bible and offers spiritual insights about the *I* within us. That we are created in the image of God, as beings of a divine nature, underlies the basic precepts of Part I of this book. These articles express the discoveries I have made along my lifelong spiritual journey.

OUR SPIRITUAL JOURNEY

We are all on a spiritual journey, whether we know *who* we are or *that* we are or not. This journey is inward, not outward; nobody can take it for us. Although our spiritual journey is inward, unseen, how we live our lives reflects our spirit. Therefore, reviewing our lives and contemplating our character can shed light on what direction we are taking on our inward journey.

In such contemplation, we may consider our strengths and weaknesses, successes and mistakes, and the fruits of our relationships. And, as though a map of our past stretched before us, we may follow our footprints: "What were the most important decisions I have made in my life, and where have they taken me? How have they changed my life and shaped who I am today?"

Such a review of our character and life is fundamental to becoming more aware of our divine nature. For if we can see our footprints on our inward journey, we may discover the *I* who walks in them.

Some people resist such introspection because they fear who they are inside. They would instead continue to think of themselves only regarding their roles and relationships with others, as the young woman above observed. We cannot escape who we are, but our very own divine inner being should not frighten us.

The fear of facing oneself often relates to forgiveness issues, and we all have such issues throughout our lives. Occasionally, I hear someone declare they have always quickly and easily forgiven anyone who has wronged them throughout their entire life. Perhaps in small matters, that is true, but I believe those people are deceiving themselves in making such a statement. If forgiving others were that easy for even one person on earth, then Jesus sacrificed his life in vain.

Along our spiritual journey, we cannot get around forgiveness or jump over it or slither under it. Forgiveness is a doorway, and the only way to truly attain peace in our hearts and spiritual freedom is to pass through its door.

While no set course in life teaches us how to forgive, spiritual learning comes from our personal experiences and various other sources. The experiences of others can be invaluable. Part II of this book, "A Story of Forgiveness," recounts a remarkable story that happened in my own life along my spiritual journey. This story is here to awaken us to a much deeper meaning of Christianity than what we know it as today.

Now, I testify that Part II, "A Story of Forgiveness," is an entirely true story, and I am the one who wrote every word. However, the powerful message that emerged from the story as I wrote it far surpasses the capabilities of my imagination. For this, I give full credit to the loving light that guided me in writing Part II.

Daddy once made a very passionate wish that one day, he and I, together, would have a way to tell the whole world about Jesus. Years later, one day, out of the blue, he told me a very unusual story about a certain lady in his neighborhood when he was a boy. Afterward, he thought for a moment, and quite bewildered, he said, "Huh! I don't even know what made me think to *tell* you about that lady, Donna! In my entire lifetime, I never told a single soul about her, not even your mother, and I told her *everything*. And now, for some strange reason, I just told *you*. I have no idea *why!*"

He pondered this mystery further, shaking his head and saying quietly to himself, "Why... did I just *tell* you... that?"

We truly do not realize how God speaks through us in our ordinary conversations. Daddy was talking from his spirit about what I would write in this book, for his wish to come true, here, today. As I wrote Part II, "A Story of Forgiveness," he was that guiding and loving light.

Conventions Used in this Book

Our Creator is devoid of form and shape far beyond our perception of human gender. Yet, because of our limited minds and language, we still attempt to fit the concept of God into a male/female identity. The Holy Bible, written thousands of years ago, contains Christian language that predominantly refers to God in masculine terms, such as Father, King, Lord, etc., and pronouns such as he, his, and him. Today, many prefer more liberating, genderless names for God, such as the Divine Spirit, the Universal Source, and many others.

Various Bible translations have incorporated gender-neutral terminology over the years, but many verses remain unchanged. In Matthew 6:9, for instance, Jesus, the Son of God, instructs us: "Pray then in this way: Our Father in heaven, hallowed be your name." And Isaiah 9:6 refers to Jesus as "Wonderful Counselor, Mighty God, Everlasting Father, Prince of Peace."

Names and titles in the Bible have prophetic meanings beyond identifying people. And names for God signify specific attributes of the deity. For example, God appears to Daniel as a very old judge: "An Ancient One took his throne, his clothing was white as snow, and the hair of his head like pure wool" (Dan 7:9b–c).

The difference between God as our Father and a gender-neutral title such as the Divine Spirit is that a father implies a warm relationship, as in a family, whereas a divine spirit suggests specific sacred attributes. We are children of our Father, to whom Jesus instructed us to pray, and spirits created with the essence of the Divine Spirit.

I know God is neither a "he" nor a "she," but because of the confines of our language in the scriptures from which I draw my inspiration, I often use male-gender terms. I use "God," an all-encompassing title that many accept, to mean "God/Goddess." And rather than "it," I use "he" to mean "he/she." I use these terms to maintain the natural flow of reading in an easy story format and to prevent readers from straying from the message by having fleeting ideas about God's gender. The names or pronouns that readers prefer or identify with may be substituted if they find this objectionable. I may use liberating names occasionally, when appropriate, within the context of the subject. No one

God-naming convention will satisfy every reader, and our Creator is too great to describe in our limited language.

In this book, I do not intend to provoke controversy, engage in a debate for its own sake, or challenge anyone's religious convictions. Nor do I require anyone to agree with my spiritual or historical interpretations of the Holy Bible, though I hope they may inspire new growth. My biblical interpretations reflect my humble opinions and what I have found true. No single person holds all the answers to life's mysteries, and I do not claim to be the ultimate authority on any spiritual matter whatsoever. In summary: "Let all be fully convinced in their own minds" (Rom 14:5b).

CHAPTER 2

THE ROSE GARDEN VISION

The best place to seek God is in a garden.
You can dig for him there.
—George Bernard Shaw

AS I BEGIN TO DRIFT OFF to sleep, I come upon a beautiful, gated rose garden. Large pink and white roses are peeking through the gate.

As I walk through the big, black iron gate, I am elated by the heavenly scent of lovely flowers everywhere. Right away, I know what to do with all the pretty roses.

A man is standing in the garden on the other side of a tall cluster of rose bushes where I am. Although I cannot see his face, his identity is not important; his purpose is to help me.

From a basket containing garden tools—like clippers, pruners, and scissors—I hand a few items to the man through the rose bushes. "Here, I'll show you what people do with roses. These will make beautiful headdresses. We can make tiaras out of them for ourselves. And we'll make some for the beautiful, young maidens, who are wearing flowery island dresses, and dancing at a wedding."

Seven beautiful young maidens, all wearing tiaras, are lining up in a row and dancing at a large wedding. Their flowery island dresses are gently blowing in the breeze.

I cut some branches from the bushes to form a circled wreath while the man watches my demonstration. We start, then, to make our wreaths.

Then, I take handfuls of soft rose petals strewn all over the ground and wrap them around my wreath. The petals stick all by themselves.

Through the bushes, I can see the man's wreath is still bare; the petals are not sticking to his as they do so easily to mine. Every time he tries to wrap the rose petals around his wreath, they slide off.

I go back to admiring my beautiful tiara, now abundant with pink and white rose petals. I put the wreath on my head as I look over at the man.

"See? We made tiaras."

And it is Jesus standing there, holding his barren wreath.

"Yes... and you got to wear the flowers that time, and I got to wear the thorns."

CHAPTER 3

TRUTH

> Ask, and it will be given you; search, and you will
> find; knock, and the door will be opened for
> you. For everyone who asks receives, and
> everyone who searches finds, and for everyone
> who knocks, the door will be opened.
> —Luke 11:9-10

MANY PEOPLE FORM their beliefs based on the opinions of others, religions, traditions, and even slogans or superstitions. In shaping their spiritual beliefs, they turn to external sources for answers without ever considering asking God for the truth.

Churches, people, and books can *guide* you to an extent, but your spiritual journey is unique; only you take its path. Nobody knows better than God—and you—what is right for you. After all, is there any single religion, church, group, or person in the world that holds the undisputed truth of the fullness of the Omniscient Spirit (i.e., the one of all knowledge)?

Clinging to certitude for its own sake, religious dogmas, or rigid traditions, is unwise. Rather than becoming a convert to the beliefs of others, which may or may not be true, it is better to form your own.

God will respect whatever you judge to be so, whether it is accurate or not. You cannot receive spiritual knowledge, however excellent and trustworthy, if you have already filled your mind with borrowed opinions. If you think you already know the answers, even if your answers are false, your self-certainty will block the channels from God, the one of all knowledge.

Therefore, before judging a spiritual matter, it is wise to ask God first. Keep an open mind; do not limit spiritual answers to your own restricted beliefs or those of others. Spiritual truths will align with what God wishes to reveal, even if they may overturn your assumptions.

The sincere spiritual seeker will base their beliefs on knowledge, not ignorance or conventional opinion. As the French author André Gide once advised, "Believe those who seek the truth, doubt those who find it; doubt all, but do not doubt yourself."

ASKING GOD QUESTIONS

Some people think it is disrespectful to ask God questions. Once, when I told a friend that I ask God questions all the time, she gasped, utterly confounded. To her, it was perfectly acceptable to lean on others for spiritual answers but to stay apart from God.

God never ordained that we should wait around in ignorance until we die; thereupon, like a big surprise, he will solve all the spiritual riddles we have wondered about all our lives. Why would God keep spiritual knowledge from us now? And if we cannot have this wisdom, who is it for?

Jesus instructs us: "Love the Lord your God with all your heart, and with all your soul, and with all your mind" (Matt 22:37). Our God would not give such a command and then say, "By the way, don't ask me anything!" We should intimately know our God, the one we are to love with our whole being.

And why should it be acceptable to ask God to answer our prayer requests but not our questions? People ask God for things all the time: healing, new jobs, financial help, and better relationships. If we only ask God to fix our problems and give us things, and never ask for spiritual understanding, we risk being like the teenage boy who asks Daddy for car keys while caring little for a loving and trustworthy relationship.

Many people know *about* God but do not honestly know him beyond a faint connection, if any. God may be some version of the Ancient One for them, like a distant relative, their great, great Uncle Gus.

Such people know they *have* an Uncle Gus, and they know a few facts about him. Like, he is on their father's side, a slightly deaf, retired judge as old as Methuselah, who always dresses in dark suits and lives way across the city. But who is Uncle Gus, really? We cannot say we love God if we do not know him.

Scriptures affirm God wants us to seek spiritual knowledge. God will give us spiritual illumination, but we must do more than wonder casually—we must ask and be ardent to receive. The more questions we ask, the more we will feel God's presence through the answers.

God does not answer audibly but in many other ways, such as speaking to us through our inner voice, synchronicities, or miracles (as they might be). Some answers may come from our experiences, people, the Holy Bible or other books. When they do come, it will not require asking others what we should or should not believe. It is pretty simple: if we want an answer, we can ask God a question. He will always answer us.

SPIRITUAL DISCERNMENT

Spiritual discernment, ultimately, is the ability to think biblically about all areas of life and how God helps us reach the best decision. Discernment is making careful and wise distinctions in our thinking to decide between truth and error, or right and wrong, before making judgments.

The world is laden with Christians who lack this gift of the Holy Spirit because they do not ask for it or have misconceptions about it. We might think cult leaders, or some deceitful, mighty ministers, are the only false prophets—those of whom many scriptures warn us. Still, false prophets are also some well-meaning Christians who mislead others because they assume they already know spiritual truths without asking God or consulting the Bible. An open invitation is in James 1:5: "If any of you is lacking in wisdom, ask God, who gives to all generously and ungrudgingly, and it will be given you." In my early days as a Christian, I had to ask God for the truth about a matter.

I was 21 when I heard talk about speaking in tongues on a television ministry. So, I asked some seemingly knowledgeable Christians to inform me about this mystical subject. It was as if I could only decide what to believe by going around asking people of certain faiths what they believed. Then, I would choose to which group I belonged.

My neighbor, a very passionate Christian woman who attended an evangelical church, declared, "Speaking in tongues is the only proof you *have* that the Holy Spirit is inside of you! You *have* to speak in tongues!" Days later, two devout Christian men from another denomination reflected on my same spiritual questions. In contrast to my neighbor, they strictly warned, "Speaking in tongues is of the *devil!* Stay away from it! There are many false prophets out there!"

Which opinion was the truth? Contrary to my neighbor's unyielding stance, why should we require God to give us proof (by tongues) of the Holy Spirit? And if the men were wrong, they may be dangerously blaspheming the Holy Spirit and misleading others as well.

After pondering these two opposite positions, I concluded neither was correct. All the people involved who weighed in on the question of speaking in tongues likely formed their beliefs the same foolish way as I had, starting: they derived their beliefs from the beliefs of others and conformed to their group's consensus (or "group-think").

A faithful Christian follows Jesus, which does not mean Christians should all think the same way—as a group—on every issue. Nothing is "of God" or "of the devil" automatically because someone else, or even the majority, holds such beliefs. Blanket judgments—as if things are black or white and good or bad—only stunt our spiritual growth, and we risk becoming false prophets.

After getting two extremely conflicting answers about speaking in tongues, I decided to always go straight to the Omniscient Spirit instead of letting others convince me or impose their questionable beliefs on me that I may disagree with. God gives us the gift of spiritual discernment through our inner voice, alerting us when something does not feel right, but the noise of conventional opinion and unexamined beliefs will drown it out if we consent. When we hear that voice, we can pray to God to lead us to the truth and use the Bible as our guide.

I would rather wait forever for the answer from the Omniscient Spirit than follow others' false beliefs. As Jesus confirmed: "You will know the truth, and the truth will make you free" (John 8:32).

Chapter 4

Spirituality

The LORD God made garments of skins for the man and for his wife, and clothed them.
—Gen 3:21

SUPPOSE WHEN YOU awaken tomorrow, you look in the mirror and notice you are invisible. Would you still be alive?

Of course, you would be. You are not the temporary body made of skin and bones; the real you is your eternal soul. Your body, fit for this third dimension, is merely the vehicle for your soul, which is who you really are.

To illustrate the relationship between body and soul, think of a car. You do not *become* the car when you get behind the wheel; instead, you are the driver, operating and driving your vehicle. While you may believe you are a body and have a soul, the truth is that you are a soul experiencing life in a body. You have a body (in this lifetime).

OUR INNER WORLDS

The following paraphrases an article I read some years ago. If I ever find it again, I would love to cite and credit its author.

Only the creator can fully explain its creation; to understand something totally, one must be above it and see it as a whole. Therefore, no one field of science or philosophy has ever thoroughly explained who we are as human beings, for we are not our creators. Science and philosophy instead describe what human beings have discovered about human beings.

The third dimension is the world of physical reality, where the physical senses can perceive and the sciences can measure. In the third dimension, our brain constitutes the physical locus for our thought activity. However, the mind, where we think our thoughts, belongs to an invisible realm in the fourth dimension. The "mind" is just a word to define the holding tank for our thoughts. No single field of science can prove our invisible mind exists, nor can any philosophy verify the reality of the unseen soul.

A brain surgeon can open a patient's head to inspect the brain's complexity, including networks of nerves and the blood. The surgeon can also detect the patient's brain activity with sophisticated monitoring devices. Yet, even the most intelligent brain surgeon in the world cannot perceive a single thought of the patient. The surgeon can access the patient's physical brain's contents but not the invisible mind's thoughts.

Likewise, a heart surgeon can open a patient's chest for open-heart surgery, touch the heart muscle and valves, and see the blood. The surgeon can also get some facts about the patient's beating heart with high-tech equipment. Yet, even the greatest heart surgeon on earth cannot feel a single human emotion in the patient's heart. The emotional heart belongs to another world inside, in another dimension.

The article reminds us of how little we know about the vast and endless supernatural worlds within us. To where do these worlds lead, and how far do they go? The only evidence of their existence is our ability to think and feel.

BODY, SOUL & SPIRIT

Many believe our soul and spirit are the same entity, but they are not. God, the Divine Spirit, breathes life into our souls: "The LORD God formed man of the dust of the ground, and breathed into his nostrils the breath of life; and man became a living soul" (Gen 2:7 KJV).

Our body, soul, and spirit are intertwined. We feel our passions and desires through our body-soul connection. Our soul encapsulates our ego, personality, intellect, emotions, beliefs, and free will. Throughout the Bible, the emotional soul rejoices, grieves, loves, hates, trembles, and cries out to God. When pondering his death, Jesus mused: "Now my soul is troubled" (John 12:27a).

Our free will, governed by our powerful ego, is the most crucial aspect of our soul. Our soul determines our destiny through the decisions we make. Taking the car analogy a step further, God provides us with the car and keys (i.e., everything we need) to take our personal journey, and we should drive responsibly. The fourth book of the Maccabees 2:21–22 so eloquently states this: "When God fashioned human beings, he planted in them emotions and inclinations, but at the same time he enthroned the mind among the senses as a sacred governor over them all."

Our soul seeks pleasure and fulfillment through our physical and emotional senses in relationships, animals and nature, material items, entertainment, wealth, careers, prestige, etc. Such earthly pleasures are enjoyable, but when we expect people or things to make us happy or satisfy us, ultimately, we often end up disappointed or empty. New cars get old, designer clothes wear out, a chosen career may lead to regret, and relationships often end in heartache or loss.

Worldly things are temporal and often only false substitutes for eternal, spiritual needs. Discontentment, a longing to fill a void, and not understanding our true purpose are symptoms of a spiritual deficiency; "soul searching" is a spiritual quest. Isaiah 26:9a reveals how our soul searches for spiritual fulfillment during times of darkness: "My soul yearns for you in the night, my spirit within me earnestly seeks you." Only a close spiritual relationship with God can fulfill our soul searching.

Our spirit is at the very core of our being. While we may easily understand our body-soul connection, our soul-spirit relationship is less distinguishable. When Adam and Eve fell from grace, what was once the Lord's bright and shining light within them had gone dark; the original sin had impaired the divine spirit in humanity.

When our soul does not find fulfillment in the outer, earthly world, we turn to our inner world to find our spiritual light, seeking to shine for the Lord once again. As

Proverbs 20:27 states: "The human spirit is the lamp of the LORD, searching every inmost part."

Our divine spirit awakens when we pray to God to direct us on our path. We discover our true purpose and experience deep contentment, and the Lord keeps his heartfelt promise to us: "For surely I know the plans I have for you, says the LORD, plans for your welfare and not for harm, to give you a future with hope. Then when you call upon me and come and pray to me, I will hear you. When you search for me, you will find me; if you seek me with all your heart" (Jer 29:11–13).

Chapter 5

Beliefs & Faith

All things can be done for the one who believes.
—Mark 9:23b

OUR SPIRITUALITY INFLUENCES our thinking and behavior, and how we live our life reflects the quality of our spirituality. A belief is to "be life" of something, whatever that may be. A belief emerges from a yearning for a truth in the heart. The heart sends its message to the brain, so one may be the life of that truth by living it. Indeed, believing means to "be living" according to the heart.

Many people have opinions (or thoughts) about certain spiritual truths without holding them to be sacred or true (or as originating from God). Opinions or mere thoughts are not beliefs. Only impulses that compel us from the heart to live by some principle and act accordingly define our true beliefs. We demonstrate our faith in something by acting on our beliefs.

And although we see the world through our physical senses, what we believe about a situation, ourselves, or others affects what we consider reality. By looking at life through an optimistic lens, we will have a better experience overall.

Our mind has tremendous power, and we can change it at will. A change of mind brings about a different view. As author Wayne Dyer discovered, "Change the way you look at things, and the things you look at change."

Some assume that changing their mind about a person or situation requires effort. They show their assumption by saying, "I will *try* to think about him [or her or it] differently." The word "try" makes the process seem difficult. For example, you can *try* to lift your arm or simply lift your arm, right? Just as we can change our minds about how we see others and situations, we can also change how we see ourselves. Even lifting your arm requires faith; you must believe (even subconsciously) that you can do it.

FAITH

Our faith in God increases as we advance spiritually, and there is always room for more. When a friend once warned me, "Don't get your hopes up," for my faith that something good will come, I protested. "What is the worst that might happen to me if I do? Will I have a mental collapse or something?" "Well, no," she admitted. Then I shared Hebrews 11:1: "Faith is the assurance of things hoped for, the conviction of things not seen."

Some people are ashamed to admit that they lack faith, but many renowned biblical figures, such as Abraham, Moses, and the apostles, struggled with faith at various times. Asking God to help increase our faith is acceptable and even encouraged. We express our yearning for a closer relationship with God by praying for faith.

When Jesus performed miracles, he frequently stated such wonders happen according to one's faith. For example, Matthew 9:29–30a recounts when he healed two men of their blindness: "He touched their eyes and said, 'According to your faith let it be done to you.' And their eyes were opened."

IMAGINATION

Our imagination is the *eye of our faith*. God desires us to take part in creating our world, and being made in his *image,* he gives us the powerful tool of *imag*ination. God-given imaginations initially conceived everything from the ships that sail the oceans to the buttons on a shirt. We see the potential outcomes of our ideas, desires, and beliefs through our imagination.

PRAYING WITH IMAGINATION

Praying can take many forms, and each approach has its merits. Singing a spiritual song might inspire praise, and writing a letter to God may open our hearts. Our beliefs and emotions are always essential in whatever method we pray; they are reciprocal and affect the outcome.

Using our imagination as we pray for a specific request increases our faith. When we imagine something happening, we feel excited it could be true. Jesus instructs us to pray accordingly: "Whatever you ask for in prayer, believe that you have received it, and it will be yours" (Mark 11:24).

Sometimes, when we ask God to answer a prayer request, we do not realize we may be subconsciously asking for something else. For example, suppose you wish to find a new job and simply pray, "Lord, please help me find a new job." However, praying for something to occur in the future may never happen because the future never comes. A prayer that postpones results until the future may be from a vision of lack and constrained by fear. Since you do not already have the job of your request today, you may reinforce your fears and deprived feelings by concentrating on the *lack* of what you desire.

A more effective way to pray is with faith, gratitude, and confidence. As Jesus taught, believe God has already answered your prayer. The positive emotion of gratitude resonates at a much higher frequency than the negative emotion of fear, which will only bring you more of what you already fear. So, in the example of praying for a new job, begin by reflecting upon the things you now appreciate in your life. With heartfelt gratitude, thank God for all you have today.

Then, be somewhat specific about the job you want. If you pray vaguely for "a new job," you could wind up with any old job. So, tell God about a few features or benefits you would like in your new position. What pay do you reasonably expect, for instance, or maybe you need a job in a convenient location, or certain hours to accommodate your family's schedule?

Next, tell God what you wish to give back after receiving the new position. Perhaps you will have more time to spend with your family or volunteer in your community. What kind of employee will you commit to being?

After contemplating your wishes for your new job, now imagine you have stepped into the future. You see yourself in the answered prayer; you are in your new position. Imagine a friendly manager greeting you on your first day or how your workplace looks. How do you feel while working on your first assignment?

It is essential to feel the emotions the scene stirs up in your imagination and to believe in the reality of what you desire in your heart: you are confident, enthusiastic, happy, relieved, and excited.

As you still occupy the future in your imagination, you look out the window of your new workplace and reflect on your day. Remembering the days when you did not have such a fantastic job, now you have it. Gratitude fills your heart as you thank God for answering your prayer.

Some people believe we should only pray once for something, but this is false. The more you pray and imagine your request, the more you will feel and believe it, and the more it will solidify to become your new reality. By thanking God often for what you have and for answering your prayer, you will be in an attitude of gratitude, your faith will increase, and God will match your expectations.

HOW IMAGINATION AFFECTS OUR LIFE

Our imagination does work to shape our reality, and to some people, that may sound hard-hearted. In some cases, for instance, it may be inexplicable why one person has multiple diseases and another miraculously heals. People do have health problems, and the best we can do when sick is to take care of ourselves and reduce stress. And sometimes, we all need a friend for some advice or just to listen, but we should keep a positive frame of mind as much as possible.

While there are no cut-and-dried answers regarding the mysteries of life, sometimes we do not have to look far to recognize how some people create their adversities or contribute to them through their beliefs, thoughts, and words. An acquaintance once told me of her many afflictions: she had just broken out in a mysterious rash; she could barely walk because of a knee problem; her arthritis had been terrible lately, and her medicine was no longer working. To top it all off, a cyst was now growing (which the doctors could not diagnose).

The more this feeble woman dwelled on her maladies, the more she had of them and the worse they got. There was no stopping her complaints, and she trumped every positive suggestion with a bigger disorder. As hard as I tried to offer a broader arena of favorable possibilities outside the narrow confines of her suffering, she insisted on repeating and adding to her growing list of ailments.

Then she announced her disappointment in God. "I pray all the time. I keep asking God for help with all these things, but God doesn't want to help me. He doesn't care. I think I'm supposed to live like this forever."

How can this sick person expect God or doctors to make her diseases disappear while she puts all her energy into keeping them actively alive? And by praying with no faith in God, and in such lack, she answers her own prayers to "live like this forever."

In contrast to such self-perpetuated pain, some self-induced remedies may ease our miseries. When doctors diagnosed American journalist Norman Cousins with a fatal disease, they gave up on him. They sent him home with several months to live.

Cousins had long believed there was a link between human emotions and physical health. He found a doctor who would work with him at his home, and as a team, they implemented his healing strategy to regain his health. Cousins discovered that ten-minute spells of laughter, sparked by the television show *Candid Camera* and various humorous films, provided two-hour periods entirely free from pain. Within several months, he healed.

Norman Cousins' remarkable story stunned his doctors and the medical community, and inspired many research projects. Cousins recounts how he beat the odds in his book, *Anatomy of an Illness, as Perceived by the Patient,* which was also made into a movie.

WORRISOME THOUGHTS

Of course, bad things happen in life, and we cannot deny their existence. We must take the best action to handle them and ease our worrisome thoughts.

To worry is to imagine that a current situation will cause an adverse event to come. When we worry, we are projecting a negative picture of what might happen next. But this has not happened yet because our worries are in the future. We often imagine a negative outcome first, but we may instead imagine what a positive result might look like in the same situation. Jesus' sound advice also helps in those times: "Do not worry about tomorrow, for tomorrow will bring worries of its own" (Matt 6:34).

CONCLUSION

What we think, say, believe, and imagine are living energies that attract the target of our focus. They alter our moods and determine our capacity to feel joy or sadness, pleasure or pain, and confidence or fear. Understanding how to use our powerful imagination and how our words and beliefs affect us can improve our lives. This type of reflection helps us grow spiritually and to identify where we might ask God to help us deepen our faith.

CHAPTER 6

WAS JESUS ON THE BUS?

One God and Father of all, who is above all and
through all and in all.
—Eph 4:6

WHEN I WAS SEVEN, I listened to my older sisters marveling at a story one of them had heard. It went something like this:

A man died, and when he got to the pearly gates of heaven, God asked him why he did not help Jesus. God had sent Jesus to the man repeatedly when he needed help. Why did the man do nothing?

The man replied, "When, Lord? I never even saw him! Surely, I would have helped *Jesus* if he asked!"

So, God explained how Jesus had appeared to the man once as a hungry beggar and then once as a sick person in a hospital. Another time, Jesus appeared on a bus as someone who needed a little money. God said every time Jesus appeared to the man needing help, he turned him away.

As my sisters discussed the story, they said things like, "You better be careful! You never know where Jesus will show up!" And, "You never know if Jesus is really gonna be in that one or not!"

My sisters all speculated with fear, as though they contemplated God would take every chance to trick people— like, God sits up in the sky and sends Jesus down as his undercover cop to make random surprise appearances, disguised as impoverished strangers. Why would God be so conniving as that? And play such tricks on us?

The logic of my sisters baffled me. My second-grade teacher had been preparing me for my First Holy Communion. Throughout the school year, she kept repeating that we should treat others like Jesus is in *every* person, not just in some. I certainly did not want to believe God would send Jesus down to go around tricking people, as if waiting for us to mess up.

This story about Jesus echoes the Japanese tale, "Folklore of the Stranger: A Consideration of a Disguised Wandering Saint." A wandering saint with helpful magical powers disguises himself as a filthy beggar, walks through a village, and tests how the people might treat him. The folk tale warns us to treat strangers cautiously and not to be rude to filthy beggars or throw stones at them because they may be princes in disguise.

Such age-old stories about Jesus in disguise and retold in various ways might provoke self-centered or selfish concerns in some people. What if a particular person really *had* been Jesus, and we had not helped Jesus, the Lord? (Never mind that the beggar went away hungry and could have even *died*. Shouldn't we be caring toward this man, the beggar, himself?) We worry about what might happen if that beggar really had been Jesus in disguise, and we failed to feed him. We fret over what will happen to *us* when we meet our maker if we are caught.

Whatever version of the story one may have heard, its roots are most likely in the Holy Bible, in the parable of the sheep and the goats.

THE SHEEP AND THE GOATS

The parable of the sheep and the goats (i.e., The Judgment of the Nations) is in the Gospel of Matthew 25:31–46. Many people find this narrative confusing on the surface. Therefore, a closer look at the lesson will shed light on its underlying significance.

Depicting the day of judgment, Jesus explains that the Lord will separate people into two categories of animals: sheep and goats. When people retell the story—as my sisters did—they usually wish to identify with the sheep, not the goats. Nobody wants to wind up a goat.

Jesus says the Lord will bless the sheep, and they will inherit the kingdom because they fed the Lord when he was hungry; gave him a drink when he was thirsty; welcomed him when he was a stranger; clothed him when he was naked; took care of him when he was sick; visited him when he was in prison.

When the sheep ask when they have done such things to the Lord: "The king will answer them, 'Truly I tell you, just as you did it to one of the least of these who are members of my family, you did it to me'" (v. 40).

Next, Jesus describes the judgment of the goats for not helping the Lord on the same list of human needs. The

Lord will curse the goats and send them into the eternal fire prepared for the devil and his angels.

When the goats ask when they have not done any of those things to the Lord: "He will answer them, 'Truly I tell you, just as you did not do it to one of the least of these, you did not do it to me'" (v. 45).

ARE WE A SHEEP OR A GOAT?

Now, I don't know about you, but (if I read accurately), I would likely have put myself in goat status a long time ago. The parable says if I did not do a good thing to even one of the least of these, then—hard as I try—the Lord might not let me through those pearly gates.

Let's face it. None of us are perfect. Not one of us is a purebred sheep or goat, and we will never be in our present human form. Throughout our lives, we are all varying degrees of both the sheep and the goat.

I do not always donate to beggars standing at red lights and asking for money. Sometimes I do, but not always. I admit. And when I hear about sick people, I do not always make a point to visit them, even today. Again, sometimes I do, but not every time. I hear about people getting sick all the time, though. Should I visit every one of them, even if they are not very close to me? Where do I draw the line in how much I help or give to others and to whom?

Now, there was a time when I answered a prisoner's request for a pen pal on a Christian radio station. His name was Larry, and he was in a Louisiana prison for 18 years for armed robbery. I even faithfully wrote to him for a very long time. I did my best to uplift Larry in his dreadfully bleak existence in captivity. His return letters, filled with sincere gratitude for simply being his friend, continually inspired me to write to him again. Besides writing to Larry, though, I have never approached a prison to ask if some criminal inside wants a visit. Have you?

Surely, I am not alone here. How do we live up to God's expectations? Should we just hope for a sheep's score on our heavenly report card so we get to stay up there in heaven with God? I do not think perfecting our holy report card will get us through those gates.

So, is Jesus saying God records all of our works to judge us as if we are doing favors for God? No, I do not believe God needs us to do him favors. This parable must be more than a lesson about sharing. ("God wants to teach us all to share," some might conclude.)

THE KEY IN THE PARABLE

Jesus used two animals to illustrate how the Lord will separate and judge us. However, he could have just said the Lord will divide us into groups of righteous and unrighteous people. And since there is no middle group, he will put us in one or the other.

Jesus used animals, sheep and goats, in particular, to equate their behavior to the two opposing natures in human beings. We have a divine spiritual nature and an ego nature, and we must decide which rules our lives. The sheep in the parable are righteous and choose their spiritual nature, while the unrighteous goats prefer their ego nature. Indeed, our spiritual and ego nature are two different animals.

Sheep (animals) are typically known to be gentle and peaceful. They follow their shepherd and stay with the flock for safety, guidance, and belonging. Sheep need their shepherd's loving care and protection. Without their shepherd's guidance, sheep can become lost.

The sheep are those who follow Jesus. We find confirmation that he is the shepherd in Hebrews 13:20: "The God of peace, who brought back from the dead our Lord Jesus, the great shepherd of the sheep, by the blood of the eternal covenant."

The sheep exhibit Christlike qualities in their daily lives. They are gentle, peaceful, and kind-hearted people. They naturally reach out to help others and acknowledge God is in every one of "the least of these." The sheep selflessly share their gifts from the Lord whenever they can. Their love and compassion reveal their living faith in Jesus Christ.

In contrast to sheep (animals), we typically know goats for having wild, unfettered behavior. Goats are notorious for butting their handlers and exhibiting a rebellious, chaotic, self-reliant attitude.

The goats are those who disregard or reject Jesus and his teachings. They are hesitant to help those in need and treat them with contempt; they do not consider how their selfish actions also harm the Lord. Their ego's self-interest demonstrates their disbelief in God, as their only hope is in their possessions and the things of this temporary world.

The mindset of the goat is that it is absurd to suppose Jesus could be in any of "the least of these," and thus, they should treat everyone with kindness. They would think that if Jesus really were in one random person on the bus, God must be testing them. The goats do not believe they need God or Jesus Christ, and they go their own way.

CONCLUSION

Heaven is a sacred and peaceful place. In our divine spiritual nature, we must follow Jesus in this life to enter heaven. When the lives of those following Jesus end, they will continue to follow him into the next life. They will have reached their final destination and be with Jesus eternally in heaven.

Heaven belongs to the Lord. People who live in their ego nature in this life are on a different path. The ego nature is a foreign entity to the divine spirit. The Lord will not accommodate their selfishness or settle their arguments in heaven. When the lives of those living in their ego nature end, the Lord will not suddenly embrace them if they never knew him. On Judgment Day, they also will continue to reach their final destination.

We seem to approach the parable by asking, "How will the Lord judge me?" as if only the Lord will decide our eternal destiny. Yet, the Lord gives us the free will to decide for ourselves: "Before each person are life and death, and whichever one chooses will be given" (Sir 15:17). We may choose to either follow Jesus in this life, the Great Shepherd, or reject him and go our own way.

CHAPTER 7

WHERE IS GOD?

If you picture God only existing outside of
yourself, as the up-in-the-sky god, or like "He's
up there, I'm down here," then you have the
wrong god. And if you do not see God in
others, then you have the wrong god.
—Neville Goddard

THE VERSE IN MATTHEW 25:40 is: "Truly I tell you,
just as you did it to one of the least of these who are
members of my family, you did it to me." Yet some versions
of the Bible interpret the verse as "you did it *for* me."

Doing something *to* God is not the same as doing
something *for* God. The word "to" indicates only two: you
and God; you are doing something directly to God.
However, "for" can mean three: you, the beggar, and God.
You can do something (e.g., help the beggar) for someone
(i.e., for God) in their absence, but doing something *to* them
requires their presence. Is God up in the sky then, looking

down and asking you to go help the beggar over there? Or is God present as the beggar? God *is* the beggar.

We must acknowledge God exists in *all* people, not just in some. If God is in the beggar, he must be in you, me, and all of us. For if a fair and loving God were in one of us, he would leave no one else out.

THE LIVING SPIRIT WITHIN

Some people readily accept that God is present in little children but not adults. Perhaps they believe we have a date on the calendar of our life marked, "You should have known better by now," when the living spirit of God abandons us. If the breath of God leaves us and we are still alive on earth, we will be an empty shell made of dried clay.

The word "spirit" originates from the Latin *spiritus,* which means "breath." We have a deep, innate connection to God, according to Job 27:3: "As long as my breath is in me, and the spirit of God is in my nostrils." If our connection to God has an expiration date, I believe we would know. God never abandons us, but we abandon God.

JUDGING OTHERS

We judge others based on their words and actions for our protection and safety and those around us. Then after, we treat them according to what we know. We need to judge others for what happens here on earth, but God is the ultimate judge of the heart, spirituality, and eternal destination of all.

Nobody owns God, and we have no right to decide who among us gets him. Jesus came to abolish the "us/them" dichotomy, or anyone's authority to determine who is "in" with God and who is "out."

Some professed Christians assume that having Jesus in their life gives them the authority to quickly judge and condemn ordinary people they hardly know, and they only *hurt* those souls and drive them away. People are far more open to loving messages about Jesus than to accusatory ones that contradict his purpose: "God did not send the Son into the world to condemn the world, but in order that the world might be saved through him" (John 3:17). God does not reject or punish ordinary people because of their human nature before they fully understand that the only way to the Father is through the Son.

This path to the Father *through* the Son may be apparent to Christians who follow Jesus daily. Still, many well-meaning, ordinary people who wish to identify as Christians need help in understanding this. Many think believing in Jesus simply means acknowledging that he lived, died, and rose again, and that being a Christian means living a reasonably decent life. To them, Jesus may be more like the perfect example.

While some of these ordinary people may pray to God and even *beg* God for their requests in times of trouble, deep down, they may not feel confident he hears them. They may not understand that a true Christian must follow Jesus wholeheartedly and may not realize the importance of his message: "I am the way, and the truth, and the life. No one comes to the Father except through me" (John 14:6).

Jesus did not threaten ordinary people with an ultimatum that they would go to hell if they did not follow him. Harsh scriptures of condemnation were, and are, for those who knowingly and willfully reject his message. Jesus drew people to him with loving words, such as: "Come to me, all you that are weary and are carrying heavy burdens, and I will give you rest. Take my yoke upon you, and learn from me; for I am gentle and humble in heart, and you will find rest for your souls. For my yoke is easy, and my burden is light" (Matt 11:28–30).

A mature and understanding Christian will share the message of God's love, foremost, not one of quick judgment and condemnation. We all run *from* those who want to judge us and run *to* those who want to love us. A righteous attitude gives Christianity a bad name, and many ordinary people, who might otherwise want to know more about Jesus and how to follow him faithfully, turn away instead.

ARE WE ALL GOD'S CHILDREN?

Sometimes, when Christians try to tell others about Jesus, they face the objection that we are all God's children. Therefore, shouldn't we be content as we are without committing to follow Jesus? Do only some people need Jesus, or do some need him more than others? After all, Psalm 82:6 says: "You are gods, children of the Most High, all of you."

Yet we must also consider Romans 9:8: "It is not the children of the flesh who are the children of God, but the children of the promise are counted as descendants."

Adam and Eve were once the children of God but became children of the flesh (i.e., children of the world) when they rejected God. Then humanity began committing every transgression conceivable. Genesis 6:6 declares:

"And the Lord was sorry that he had made humankind on the earth, and it grieved him to his heart."

God reconciles with humankind in his plan of adoption. He *adopts* those who voluntarily want to be his children and show their love for him by following Jesus Christ. Ephesians 1:5 supports God's plan of adoption: "He destined us for adoption as his children through Jesus Christ, according to the good pleasure of his will." Romans 8:14–15b also speaks of adoption: "For all who are led by the Spirit of God are children of God. For you did not receive a spirit of slavery to fall back into fear, but you have received a spirit of adoption."

We do not love God because we have to but because we want to. God does not violate our free will by removing us from competing worldly desires. We can choose to love God or to live as children of the world, but God always hopes we will turn to him through his Son, Jesus Christ.

CHAPTER 8

THE IMAGE OF GOD

God created humankind in his image, in the image
of God he created them; male and female he
created them.
—Gen 1:27

G OD CREATED HUMANKIND in *his* image; both male
and female were created in God's image. Yet we tend
to make God in our own images of human beings, perhaps
based on our feelings about ourselves and our relationship
with God. When I was nine, in fourth grade, my image of
God equated to my guilty conscience after I stirred up some
trouble in school one day. It was on All Saints' Day after I
made a joke to a boy, and the joke went out of control. I was
worried sick afterward that my teacher would find out what
I did.

Sister Elena was a very petite, beautiful Filipina nun.
Always grinning from ear to ear, her exuberance was
contagious. She was also very wise, and never raised her
voice—until this happened.

During our religion lesson that day, Sister Elena asked if anyone could think of a saint's name. My friend Ray took the opportunity to get back in her good graces because she had scolded him throughout the day for mild misbehavior. Ray knew religion was my favorite subject, and he did not know any saint names. So, he whispered to ask me for the name of a saint that would please Sister Elena the *most*. I thought about God quite a bit at that age, but the devil was just a meaningless character to me, of whom I thought little. I only meant it as a little joke when I whispered back to Ray: "Lucifer."

Surely, he would know Lucifer is the devil's name because, after all, Ray was an altar boy. But before I could stop him, he jumped out of his seat, knelt in the aisle, and waved his hand to beg Sister Elena to call on him. And when she did, he sprung to his feet with a big proud smile and shouted, "Saint Lucifer!"

Mortified, Sister Elena almost fell over in front of the entire class. *"Ohh! You are so bad! Down to the principal's office you go!"* she shrieked, pointing to the door. Then Ray's mother and grandmother had to come to the school to bail him out, and they grounded him for two weeks.

Sister Elena's alarming reaction showed me how serious my blunder had been and what a terrible offense it was to pronounce the devil's name. Her response scared me so badly that I imagined my soul instantly turning pitch black. I worried I might even have to spend some time in purgatory for this one.

That night in bed, I pulled the covers over my head to hide from God. He had to be watching me, I figured. He was looking through the window by my bed from somewhere across the city, beyond the moon, and way up on top of the clouds.

God was an old man up there, with a long, flowing white beard and dressed in a black robe. He was sitting on a big throne, holding an enormous gavel. God was very distant and impersonal to me that night, an old, old, ancient judge.

A few days later, Sister Elena took me aside to recommend a good book for my book report. She thought I would really like it. We always chose our own books for our book reports, so this was quite unusual. Then when I saw the title, "Johnny Goes to Purgatory," I gulped. *God must have told her!*

My book report was about a boy who cheated on a test, then fell asleep in the classroom coat locker, and dreamed he went to purgatory for cheating. His nun teacher stood over him when he awoke, giving him important spiritual guidance about doing what is right in God's sight.

My nine-year-old experience taught me that God pays attention to *everything* I do. And he even has a planned lesson for when I mess up.

GOD IS LISTENING WITHIN

We tend to put God in faraway places and refer to him as the third person because we fashion him in our own image (typically as a male figure). Then, when we pray, we bring God closer, in the second person, as though he is present in the atmosphere. By doing so, we are no longer thinking *about* God but talking *to* him.

Yet God is closer than we ever realize. The Spirit is within us, not in the third person or the second, but in the first person. We cannot hide anything from God because he knows our hearts and hears our every thought.

Some of the earliest biblical passages prove this, such as in Genesis chapter 18, in a story about Abraham's wife, Sarah. The Lord visited Abraham outside his tent and promised him he and Sarah would have a son. Sarah was listening from inside the tent and secretly laughed to herself when she heard the Lord's promise. She did not believe it because she and Abraham were very old.

Right away, the Lord let Sarah know he heard her thoughts: "The LORD said to Abraham, 'Why did Sarah laugh, and say, "Shall I indeed bear a child, now that I am old?"'"; "But Sarah denied, saying, 'I did not laugh'; for she was afraid. He said, 'Oh yes, you did laugh'" (vv. 13, 15).

The same God you pray to is the same God within you. He is not a faraway God, as many believe, and he did not make you and then leave; God has been with you your entire lifetime, just as he is with you now. In the words of Zephaniah 3:17a: "The LORD, your God, is in your midst."

THE HOLY NAME OF GOD

We can further understand our deep connection with God by considering when he first revealed his name to humanity through Moses at the burning bush. The complete narrative appears in Exodus chapter 3.

In summary, Moses went up the mountain and noticed a bush with a blazing fire, but it was not burning down. God called out to him from the bush when he went to investigate it. He identified himself to Moses as the God of his father and his ancestors, Abraham, Isaac, and Jacob.

Then God outlined the noble mission he planned for Moses: Moses was to go to Pharoah and request that he release the 600,000 enslaved Israelites under his rule, and then Moses would lead them out of Egypt. Such a vast undertaking terrified Moses, and he was concerned the Israelites would not believe God had sent him:

> But Moses said to God, "If I come to the Israelites and say to them, 'The God of your ancestors has sent me to you,' and they ask me, 'What is his name?' what shall I say to them?" God said to Moses, "I AM WHO I AM."
>
> "This is my name forever, and this my title for all generations."
>
> —Exod 3:13–14a, 15b

"I am" is the most extraordinary and revelatory name for God. Jesus also confirmed this title: "Very truly, I tell you, before Abraham was, I am" (John 8:58). A vicious mob almost stoned Jesus for that statement.

A name defines one's identity, significance, and essence. *I* is the internal name we call ourselves, a name only for ourselves—even though we all share this name. Nobody can say *I* for us or use it to speak about us.

"I am" as a name for God suggests his innate union with us. The image of God, *I*, is at the core of our being. Therefore, whenever we declare "I am," like an echo, we proclaim the name of God.

God is the source of our self-worth, so what we say of ourselves extends to our source. To love ourselves is to love God since we bear his image. "I am loveable" means God is loveable; "I am intelligent" means God is intelligent.

Even so, to belittle or condemn ourselves is to criticize or condemn God. Let us take care in how we describe ourselves in our "I am" statements. When we label ourselves negatively, such as "I am unlovable" or "I am stupid," we also imply that God is unlovable or stupid. If God made us in his image, and we insult or criticize his works, how could such harsh sentiments please him? It would be as if we made a delicious dinner for our dear friend, and our friend told us how terrible the meal tasted. To acknowledge our goodness within is to praise God for the excellence of his creation.

Some believe thinking good things about themselves is inappropriate or arrogant. An egotistical statement or thought is one of superiority and comparison, such as "I am more beautiful [or intelligent] than you." When we elevate ourselves in such a comparison, we devalue someone else.

From a spiritual view, we do not compare ourselves to others to elevate ourselves. The spirit recognizes that our inner beauty and other positive characteristics are inherent attributes of our Creator. Reminding ourselves of our fine qualities (without comparisons) produces confidence, contentment, and other good feelings. And there is no comfort or healing in a negative or depressed state of mind.

CONCLUSION

A child's mistaken notion that we are on earth and God is a strict old judge in a far-away sky implies that God's world is outside the child's human sphere. Yet, God lets the child know he hears and understands their world.

While the expansiveness of the supernatural God is beyond human comprehension, we may take comfort in the basic fact that we are created in the image of God. We may then identify with our source, who listens within, and discover unconditional love through our connection. God wants us to love and accept ourselves and feel good about who we are. In acknowledging our self-worth, we give credit and thanks to the intimate God and lift our spirits.

CHAPTER 9

ON EARTH AS IT IS IN HEAVEN

The LORD your God is indeed God in heaven
above and on earth below.
—Josh 2:11b

HERMES TRISMEGISTUS was a great philosopher
(580–470 BC) who taught in his sacred writings that
the smaller world within us contains all the elements of the
larger universe; the microcosm reflects the macrocosm.
Going within and studying ourselves will lead us to wisdom
and understanding creation.

Genesis is one of the essential books in the Bible, yet
often misunderstood. The first few chapters give us a
deeper understanding of who we are. God reveals the
spiritual meanings of their passages when we look at their
symbolism and beyond their historical content. By
illustrating the principle, "on earth as it is in heaven," or "as
above, so below," we discover some passages are allegories
of what we may look like in spirit.

The creation account in the book of Genesis depicts the universe outside and inside of man (i.e., the human being). Striking similarities link the greater universe (as the macrocosm) to the individual human body (as the microcosm). Such links prove rather than disprove creation by design.

Science demonstrates that the neural structure of the human brain is analogous to the networked structure of the universe. The spine, the axis of the human body, resembles the earth's planetary axis. The human body is 70% salt water, and the earth's surface is 70% salt water.

Many other remarkable parallels exist between the two universes, the microcosm and the macrocosm. Albert Einstein once noted, "Everyone who is seriously engaged in the pursuit of science becomes convinced that the laws of nature manifest the existence of a spirit vastly superior to that of men."

OUR SPIRITUAL ANATOMY

The Genesis account of the greater universe also presents a view of the spiritual constituents of the human being. Genesis 1:16 states: "God made the two great lights—the greater light to rule the day and the lesser light to rule the night." The sun may represent our divine spirit as our greater light that rules our day, while the moon may represent our ego, our lesser light that rules our night.

Then, Genesis 2:8 tells us: "The LORD God planted a garden in Eden, in the east; and there he put the man whom he had formed." And, God planted our hearts in the east side of our bodies.

Genesis 2:10 continues: "A river flows out of Eden to water the garden, and from there it divides and becomes four branches." And, our blood flows through four valves that extend from our hearts.

Heaven is a place inside of you, somewhere deep within. For if God is in heaven, and if he is within, then heaven must be somewhere within you, too.

It is quite credible that Jesus described God's kingdom as being within: "The kingdom of God cometh not with observation: Neither shall they say, Lo here! or, lo there! for, behold, the kingdom of God is within you" (Luke 17:20–21 KJV).

Such scriptures do not mean we will instantly be in heaven when we die, no matter how we live. However, they imply that the only path to heaven is spiritual, through our hearts.

How Do We Tend to the Garden?

We are to care for our hearts as if cultivating our spiritual gardens in heaven. Genesis 2:15 reveals this was the Lord's intention: "The LORD God took the man and put him in the garden of Eden to till it and keep it." And Proverbs 4:23 instructs us: "Keep your heart with all vigilance, for from it flow the springs of life." Our hearts are to overflow with the fruits of the Spirit, such as kindness, gentleness, compassion, generosity, patience, and love.

But sadly, our human nature is mixed. The negative side of the ego lurks within the same garden and grows weeds of greed, selfishness, arrogance, prejudices, hatred, jealousy, and unforgiveness as its weapons. The same heart that can deeply love can just as much despise.

What happens in our hearts affects us and those around us. But the ego is too proud to see that when we hurt others, we hurt ourselves. Then, when our relationships end badly, sometimes we tell ourselves that love has broken our hearts. And we turn away from love by building walls against it, to protect ourselves from the love that might hurt us again. Love is the healer, not the culprit. So let us not blame love for that, for "God is love" (1 John 4:16b).

CHAPTER 10

ADAM AND EVE

> You may freely eat of every tree of the garden; but
> of the tree of the knowledge of good and evil
> you shall not eat, for in the day that you eat of
> it you shall die.
> —Gen 2:16-17

HAVE YOU EVER WONDERED what happened to Adam and Eve or what they did, exactly? You may have some fuzzy picture of them in a heavenly garden, only to be required to leave because they ate some mysterious fruit thousands of years ago, a fruit God had forbidden them to eat. But what does the story mean, and what does it have to do with you and me today?

Sometimes, we do not believe we are anything like the people in the Bible. We think whatever happened to them does not apply to us because they lived thousands of years ago, and we are all different now.

While making dinner one day, I asked, "Lord, I really want to know about Adam and Eve. What did they do that was so bad anyhow? I've been wondering about that one all my life."

Right away, a vision arose above me of a campfire in the rain. Billowing smoke was going down to the ground from it, and to the right was the word "DISPLEASURE" spelled out in big letters, made of smoke. This vision was a sign, like Cain's rejected offering to God.

Through my inner voice, the Lord asked, "Why do you want to know about the sins of your neighbors, Donna?" He knew my question was not for my spiritual growth or any good at all. I was just being nosey. I hoped to learn about what someone else had done wrong.

My face turned red from embarrassment, and I acted like Sarah when she laughed at God and denied it. As if God could actually be *mistaken,* I said, "Oh, no, Lord, I didn't mean it like *that.* I didn't mean it like that at *all!*"

He wasn't buying it. Flustered by his silence, I still did not want to admit my guilt. I stopped what I was doing to get my Bible and opened to the book of Genesis. I pointed to the date on the page (4004 BC) and said, "Look, Lord— those people lived 6,000 years ago! I'm not anything *like* them. I was just curious and thought the passage recounted some weird sin committed by some ancient people."

As I started back to the kitchen, I felt his presence near my shoulder. "Oh... so you're not anything like *those* people?" he asked.

I stopped.

"The picture! The picture! Show me the picture! What did they look like to you?"

As a child, I read the story of Adam and Eve many times. Strangely, I always had the same vision when I read it. Two different couples always appeared in two different worlds. So, I showed God the picture of Adam and Eve from my childhood vision after they ate the forbidden fruit.

"The *other* picture! Show me the *other* picture!" he fussed. So, I showed him the picture of Adam and Eve before they ate the fruit.

He grew silent then, to let me think about the story and my childhood vision. The vision was always so vivid, except for when I came to "the tree of life also in the midst of the garden and the tree of the knowledge of good and evil" (Gen 2:9b–c). Every time I read that verse, the words "tree of life" were blurry, vibrating, and raised above the page.

My Childhood Vision

Adam and Eve are in a peaceful, scenic garden, lush with the beauty of nature. All is crystal clear and brilliantly colorful. A gentle yellow sun rests in a soft blue sky. Vibrant flowers and exotic trees exist alongside birds, butterflies, and babbling blue brooks.

Adam and Eve are a tall and extraordinarily radiant couple with a very natural poise. They have toned and muscular bodies, golden tans, and silky brown hair to their waists. They are about 30, yet ageless. Together they walk side by side, holding hands, on a path where gentle lions, tigers, and other animals randomly emerge from the trees and follow them on their walk.

Then...

The crafty serpent appears and draws Eve's attention to the tree of the knowledge of good and evil in the middle of the garden. The serpent points out its tasty-looking fruit hanging from its branches. Eve inspects it. The fruit of this tree looks too *delicious* to be poisonous. Then the serpent claims God is keeping the truth from her, telling her not to eat it. This fruit will actually make her and Adam *wise*, like God. And they surely will *not* die! So, she and Adam eat this forbidden fruit, and...

Poof!

Now, they suddenly inhabit a colorless, gray, lifeless world. The place seems without trees, animals, water, and vegetation—there is nothing. Only a dreary, overcast sky, and a flat, gray landscape paved by scattered rock, is present. And many empty caves are lined up in a row.

At first, the couple keeps going in and out of the empty caves, scrounging for food to survive. It is too blurry to discern the features of their bodies now because they move so fast. They zoom into each cave entrance, glance around for hardly a second, then zip along to the next. From one cave to the next, in *so many caves,* they are on an endless search for food, but they find no food.

Next, they are trudging along a path of scattered rock on the bare, flat ground in front of the caves. They are in a stupor, and their eyes are half shut.

Now, Adam and Eve are short, hunched over, and very out of shape. Their thick, black, frizzy hair extends down to their knees, and they have big hooked noses and warts all over their overweight bodies. They seem to be in their 60s or so, but they look shriveled and wizened, as if they might have lived by now for thousands of years.

Adam is carrying a big club on his shoulder, and Eve is schlepping behind him. As they walk along in their stupor, they shake their heads from side to side while searching for food and bickering.

Then suddenly, arising from between the cracks in the stony gray ground, a single, bright green blade of vegetation springs up along their path. This blade is the only greenery and sign of life in their entire world. Adam walks right by without noticing the plant at all. As Eve passes by this stalk, she shakes her head in its direction, though she misses it, too.

THE MEANING OF THE VISION

And so I asked, "What does the vision mean, Lord? I never understood it as a kid."

> I sent them from the garden then,
> to go in and out of empty graves,
> from one life to the next,
> to look for what they thought they did not have,
> until they could get it right,
> and recognize the only sign of life,
> the tree of life.
> —the inner voice

The Lord revealed the parallel between the fall of Adam and Eve and my own. First, Adam and Eve were a beautiful couple in a garden of abundance. Then they fell into their ego nature when they believed the forbidden fruit would give them more, something they thought God had not given them. So, God sent them from the garden to search for what they believed God had not given them.

When the Lord first asked for the picture of Adam and Eve, I immediately showed him the picture from my ego's view—the ugly couple searching for what they thought God had not given them. The Lord fussed when he requested the second picture because the first time he asked, I should have shown him the image from my spiritual view—the beautiful couple, first in the vision, in the abundant garden God had given them.

And Adam and Eve, in their stupor, turned a blind eye to the bright green blade of vegetation springing up along their path, the only sign of life. They did not recognize the tree of life. Likewise, every time I read the story, I disregarded the "tree of life," the only wavy, vibrating words raised above the page.

Alas, Lord, I am just like *those* people, in 4004 BC.

CHAPTER 11

THE EGO NATURE

For what the flesh desires is opposed to the Spirit,
and what the Spirit desires is opposed to the
flesh; for these are opposed to each other.
—Gal 5:17

THE STORY OF ADAM AND EVE reveals the origins of
the dualistic nature of human beings. Our divine
spiritual nature and the dark side of our ego are two
opposing forces within us.

Our healthy human ego is the necessary and
beneficial element of our nature that makes us unique. In
and of itself, the ego is not bad. Our ego, our individualized
character, acts as our self-preservation mechanism; it
allows us to interact with the world, set boundaries, and
make decisions in our best interests.

However, the shady side of our ego lacks confidence
and fears losing control. The negative ego, which only
considers itself and acts out of fear, causes all wicked deeds

and destructive emotions—those poisonous weeds in the heart. This part of our ego rejects the Spirit.

Adam and Eve had been perfect and whole until they ate the forbidden fruit. Genesis chapter 2 describes a beautiful garden God had given them and dominion over all creation, including the animals. They were wealthy in every way and did not have to work. God only required them to till and keep their lovely garden. They had it all.

Then the serpent appeared and tricked Eve into becoming suspicious of God: "Did God say, 'You shall not eat from any tree in the garden'?" (Gen 3:1). As if to say, "Did God actually *say* that, though?" Then he filled her ears with dirty gossip. He claimed God had lied to her and convinced her that God desired to keep her ignorant and less grand than he was.

Eve did not know evil until she tasted it through her ego. As she stood amidst the beautiful garden God had given her, surrounded by overflowing abundance, the serpent tempted her to believe in a picture of lack. Somebody, or something, had more than she had.

It did not occur to Eve that she could be more or less than anyone or anything else—until the serpent enticed her to look through the eyes of her ego and compare herself to God. And she did not realize that she *was* God (as a child of God). God had created her in his image and likeness, and his spirit was within her.

Through her blind ego, Eve did not see herself as a god already, but as a being who would like to become one. She did not see herself as wise, but as one who must become wise. She had separated herself from the spirit of God within her in every way when she compared herself to him.

In simplest terms, the negative ego is 100% pure self, so it is concretely blind to the spirit. Through this part of the ego, one can only see themselves compared to someone else; they evaluate themselves as superior or inferior to others as if on a measuring stick. It keeps them thinking they should be greater than others and are less than the Creator has made them to be.

When making such comparisons, one must separate from those they wish to compare themselves. They must look outside themselves to see what someone else has compared to what they do not have. Then they act out of fear of lack and broken confidence. The ego is self-serving and self-centered, so it is impossible to love others when a person is in this state.

In contrast to the ego, the divine spirit sees everyone as alike and equal and neither superior nor inferior in terms of status; whether a person is a CEO or a dishwasher is of no consequence. Love alone makes up the spiritual nature, and it cannot put itself on center stage to seek attention over others.

When the serpent seduced Adam and Eve into becoming jealous of God, they had to externalize God to compare themselves to him. They could no longer love God when they fell into their self-serving ego state.

SIGNS OF THE NEGATIVE EGO

The account of Adam and Eve's downfall, found in Genesis chapter 3, identifies some of the human ego's negative aspects and the fall of humanity. When Adam and Eve believed the serpent's lie, the *nature* of the lie suddenly became *alive* in them. All the telltale signs of their negative ego instantly appeared.

They vainly attempted to cover up their guilt because they were ashamed of what they did: "Then the eyes of both were opened, and they knew that they were naked; and they sewed fig leaves together and made loincloths for themselves" (v. 7).

They hid from God because they feared him since they had disobeyed him. When the Lord called out to Adam and asked where he was, Adam (unknowingly) told on himself: "I heard the sound of you in the garden, and I was afraid, because I was naked; and I hid myself. He said, 'Who told you that you were naked? Have you eaten from the tree of which I commanded you not to eat?'" (vv. 10–11).

Then they got defensive. The guilty ego always points outward rather than admitting responsibility. When God asked them what they had done, they blamed someone else for their actions.

When God asked Adam if he had eaten the forbidden fruit, Adam pointed to God: "The woman whom you gave to be with me, she gave me fruit from the tree, and I ate" (v. 12). So, Adam said it was *God's* fault for giving him Eve, his wife. When God questioned Eve about what she had done, she blamed the serpent for enticing her: "The serpent tricked me, and I ate" (v. 13b).

The serpent was the doer of evil, who beguiled Eve into doing the first evil. It seems Eve was the first to claim, "The devil made me do it." I once read that the word "devil" originated from "doer of evil." Then "d'evil" became the contracted version. The apostrophe eventually dropped, and "devil" replaced it.

CONCLUSION

That God accommodates human beings according to what they believe is incredible. Since God created Adam and Eve in his image, their beliefs had tremendous power. The couple started wealthy but found themselves outside their lavish garden when they believed in a picture of lack: "Therefore the Lord God sent him forth from the garden of Eden, to till the ground from which he was taken" (v. 23).

God had warned them they would surely die if they disobeyed him; as divinely spiritual beings, they did. As a result, they became alive physically: "The man named his wife Eve, because she was the mother of all living" (v. 20). God covered their dormant spirits with skins and sent them to live on earth as mortals in their ego nature. They had rebelled; they ran away from God to become children of the world.

CHAPTER 12

A BIBLICAL TRAIL OF TWO NATURES

No one can serve two masters. Either you will hate
the one and love the other, or you will be
devoted to the one and despise the other.
—Matt 6:24a NIV

I HAVE ALWAYS IMAGINED our human nature to be like a tree split into two branches: the ego and the spiritual. Some biblical stories are allegories of these two opposing natures within us. When a father has two sons, his firstborn illustrates the ego nature (also known as the "son of man") while the second son symbolizes the spiritual nature (the spirit may be called the "son of God").

The first two sons of a father who exhibit our two natures appear throughout several generations in the book of Genesis. In this allegorical light, biblical stories make more sense than from a historical standpoint alone. If these accounts were solely historical, one would question why God would automatically favor one son over the other.

(The title for Jesus, the "Son of Man," represents his ennobled ego nature and does not conform to my use of the "son of man" as the ego-self, nor does my use of the "son of God" indicate the divinity of Jesus, the "Son of God.")

Adam and Eve gave birth to the conflict between our two natures when they compared themselves to God and grew jealous, yet failed to recognize that their divine spirit was God. Their inflated sense of self caused them to lose touch with their higher purpose, and their ego became a veil between them and the spirit of God within them.

Their transgression resulted in the human being's divided nature—the dominating ego and the dormant spiritual. Then Adam and Eve gave birth to two sons, one of each nature. Since their ego desired to rule over the spiritual, their firstborn son was of the ego nature, and their second son was spiritual. Then the pattern continued down through the generations.

CAIN AND ABEL

Cain and Abel, the two sons of Adam and Eve, are the subjects of Genesis chapter 4. The narrative begins by informing us that Cain is the firstborn son and Abel the second. Then we learn their occupations: "Abel was a keeper of sheep, and Cain a tiller of the ground" (v. 2b). Cain's occupation as a "tiller of the ground" means he was a farmer, a being of the earth, representing the son of man. Abel was a shepherd, symbolizing the son of God. In many biblical passages, the shepherd refers to Jesus, as he himself declared: "I am the good shepherd" (John 10:14a).

Cain and Abel each brought an offering to the Lord. Cain grew jealous when the Lord rejected his offering and accepted Abel's. So the Lord questioned Cain: "Why are you angry, and why has your countenance fallen? If you do well, will you not be accepted? And if you do not do well, sin is lurking at the door; its desire is for you, but you must master it" (vv. 6–7).

But Cain had an ego nature and could not master sin: "Cain said to his brother Abel, 'Let us go out to the field.' And when they were in the field, Cain rose up against his brother Abel, and killed him. Then the Lord said to Cain, 'Where is your brother Abel?' He said, 'I do not know; am I my brother's keeper?' And the Lord said, 'What have you done? Listen; your brother's blood is crying out to me from the ground!'" (vv. 8b–10).

Cain and Abel's story is much like Adam and Eve's. Cain rose up against Abel and killed him because he envied the son of God, who God loved. He lured Abel to the field where he thought nobody would see him murder him. Then he buried Abel in the ground to cover up his crime.

And Adam and Eve rose up and killed the son of God within them because they were jealous of God. Then they hid among the trees and covered themselves with fig leaves; metaphorically, after they killed the divine spirit within them, they buried it under (the veil of) their ego.

When the Lord asked Cain where Abel was, he got defensive and lied. He tried to blame anyone else, defiantly claiming his brother was not his responsibility ("Am I my brother's keeper?"). When the Lord asked Adam and Eve to explain their actions, they got defensive and tried to blame someone else. The Lord let Cain, and Adam and Eve, know he knew everything they had done.

Years later, Adam had a third son to carry on the seed of the son of God: "When Adam had lived one hundred thirty years, he became the father of a son in his likeness, according to his image, and named him Seth" (5:3).

ISHMAEL AND ISAAC

The next illustration of two sons born with opposing natures is Abraham's two sons, Ishmael and Isaac. Now, Abraham had such a deep love for God that God referred to him as "Abraham, my friend" (Isa 41:8). But even the most loyal prophets err as human beings, as shown in how Abraham conceived his firstborn son, Ishmael.

The account begins in Genesis chapter 15 when God promises Abraham he will have a son whom he will bless with an everlasting covenant and countless descendants. Abraham assumes the child will be born to him by a servant because Sarah is barren. However, God clarifies Abraham will have this child with Sarah, and Abraham believes him.

Years pass, and Sarah seems to have lost faith that God would ever fulfill his promise of a son for Abraham and her. So, (in chapter 16) she devises a plan for Abraham to father a child with her servant, Hagar. And although Abraham once believed in God's promise of a son with Sarah, his faith seems to have also waned. He agrees to Sarah's proposal to create a son with Hagar.

But Sarah's plan to use Hagar as a surrogate mother backfires. Hagar gets arrogant toward Sarah when she becomes pregnant because she carries Abraham's baby. Sarah then despises Hagar and blames it all on Abraham. She tells Abraham: "This is all your fault! I put my servant into your arms, but now that she's pregnant she treats me with contempt. The Lord will show who's wrong—you or me!" (16:5 NLT).

Now the situation rings of domestic quarreling, and Abraham wants to wash his hands of the mess. He tells Sarah to deal with Hagar however she chooses. So, Sarah mistreats Hagar, and Hagar runs away.

Then an angel appears to Hagar and prophesies: "You have conceived and shall bear a son; you shall call him Ishmael, for the LORD has given heed to your affliction. He shall be a wild ass of a man, with his hand against everyone, and everyone's hand against him; and he shall live at odds with all his kin" (vv. 11–12).

Abraham and Sarah seemed to have acted from the ego-natured mindset that they would create a baby on their own if God were unwilling to fulfill his promise. Their plan led to marital problems and other issues.

Still, God understood Abraham and Sarah's human frailties and waning faith. He fulfilled his promise to them 13 years later: "Sarah shall bear you a son, and you shall name him Isaac. I will establish my covenant with him as an everlasting covenant for his offspring after him" (17:19). Isaac was born the following year.

Therefore, Abraham's first son, Ishmael, was born with a rebellious, ego nature. Isaac, the son of God, received the blessings of God's everlasting covenant.

ESAU AND JACOB

Esau and Jacob, the fraternal twin sons of Isaac, also had two opposing natures. Genesis chapter 25 marks the beginning of their saga, which continues throughout and concludes with a dubious truce in chapter 33.

When Isaac's wife, Rebekah, asks why she felt struggling in her womb during her pregnancy, the Lord prophesies: "Two nations are in your womb, and two peoples born of you shall be divided; the one shall be stronger than the other; the elder shall serve the younger" (25:23).

The earthy description of Esau, the firstborn, as red and all hairy at birth reveals he embodied the ego, as the son of man. Then Jacob emerged, gripping Esau's heel, showing the son of God's desire to be first.

The texts characterize Esau as a skilled hunter and an immoral and rebellious man with little regard for his future. He purposely made life miserable for Isaac and Rebekah by marrying two godless women from Ishmael's household who worshipped false idols.

Jacob is portrayed as a shepherd, and a plain man who thought about his future. His wife, Rachel, was from Abraham's household. Jacob had spiritual interests, but he also had a cunning side.

As the eldest son, Esau was to inherit a special birthright as the family patriarch and a twofold portion of his father's inheritance (Deut 21:15–17). However, Esau did not value his birthright. Once, he went to Jacob and asked for a bowl of stew. Jacob agreed to feed him in exchange for his birthright. Esau figured it would be useless if he died of hunger anyhow, so he sold his extraordinary birthright to Jacob for a cheap bowl of lentil stew and some bread. Afterward, Esau despised his birthright.

When Isaac was near death and his vision was failing, he intended to bless Esau with his birthright. But Jacob impersonated Esau and received Isaac's blessing:

"May God give you of the dew of heaven, and of the fatness of the earth, and of plenty of grain and wine. Let peoples serve you, and nations bow down to you. Be lord over your brothers, and may your mother's sons bow down to you" (Gen 27:28–29b).

After learning Isaac had blessed Jacob, Esau begged Isaac to bless him. Still, Isaac refused, as Hebrews 12:16–17 explains: "See to it that no one becomes like Esau, an immoral and godless person, who sold his birthright for a single meal. You know that later, when he wanted to inherit the blessing, he was rejected, for he found no chance to repent, even though he sought the blessing with tears."

Esau hated Jacob because of the blessing and vowed to kill him, but Jacob fled until Esau's wrath subsided. They had a shaky reunion (in chapter 33) because Jacob did not trust Esau, and they parted ways. Although Esau did not kill Jacob, their story is another of the firstborn, the son of man, who hated the son of God.

THE PRODIGAL AND HIS BROTHER

The Gospel of Luke 15:11–32 contains a famous parable about a father and his two sons (i.e., The Prodigal and His Brother). Jesus taught such lessons to help us better understand who we are spiritually and where we stand in our relationship with our Father in heaven.

Some know this as "The Prodigal Son" or "The Lost Son," and preachers often teach it straightforwardly about the younger son who ran away from his father and then returned. From this perspective, people may find meaning in the story of a Christian who strayed from their faith and then returned.

However, this story is about recovering humanity's spiritual nature (i.e., our son of God) from its spiraling state after Adam and Eve fell. When Adam and Eve chose their ego to dominate, they spiritually ran away from God. So, although our spiritual nature is divine by design, it is flawed until we turn to our Father in heaven and ask for forgiveness.

The parable starts with the younger son, who symbolizes the wayward son of God: "There was a man who had two sons. The younger of them said to his father, 'Father, give me the share of the property that will belong to me.' So he divided his property between them. A few days later, the younger son gathered all he had and traveled to a distant country, and there he squandered his property in dissolute living" (vv. 11–13).

The younger son showed no love for his father. He was so ungrateful that he asked for his inheritance before his father even died. Then, after his father gave it to him, he quickly packed his bags and ran as far away from his father as he could get. He did not value his inheritance, but went and blew it all on an immoral, piggish lifestyle.

Then we learn that a famine broke out after the younger son had foolishly wasted his entire fortune. Out of desperation, he took a job feeding pigs to sustain himself. He was so hungry that even the pigs' slop looked appetizing, but no one gave him any of it. Then one day, while in the mud feeding the pigs, he realized his father's servants had enough to eat, and he was dying of hunger. So, he went home to beg his father to forgive him and take him back as one of his servants.

"He set off and went to his father. But while he was still far off, his father saw him and was filled with compassion; he ran and put his arms around him and kissed him. Then the son said to him, 'Father, I have sinned against heaven and before you; I am no longer worthy to be called your son'" (vv. 20–21). But the father ordered his servants to provide his son with the finest clothing, a beautiful ring and sandals, and prepare a large celebration for his homecoming.

Although we may not see ourselves as one falling to the same depths as the younger son, he illustrates what happened to the divine spiritual nature of humanity. And when we turn to our Father and ask for forgiveness, he does not punish us for our past. Instead, he quickly forgives us with love and compassion and rejoices in our homecoming.

The elder son in the parable also plays a significant role by demonstrating various facets of the ego nature. The elder son is self-righteous and does not appreciate our Father in heaven, either. Although this son was physically at home all those years, his heart was also far from his father's.

When the elder son heard the music and dancing at his brother's celebration, he was jealous and refused to attend: "Then he became angry and refused to go in. His father came out and began to plead with him. But he answered his father, 'Listen! For all these years I have been working like a slave for you, and I have never disobeyed your command; yet you have never given me even a young goat so that I might celebrate with my friends. But when this son of yours came back, who has devoured your property with prostitutes, you killed the fatted calf for him!'" (vv. 28–30).

The elder son is there to tell us that righteous works or commands out of duty will not earn us a place in heaven; simply living a decent life with an empty heart for God is not enough.

The father's answer to the elder son reiterates how our heavenly Father rejoices when the spiritual son repents: "Son, you are always with me, and all that is mine is yours. But we had to celebrate and rejoice, because this brother of yours was dead and has come to life; he was lost and has been found" (vv. 31b–32).

CONCLUSION

The first two sons in the generations following Adam and Eve—Cain and Abel, Ishmael and Isaac, and Esau and Jacob—are fundamental illustrations of the conflict between the son of man and the son of God. Each son was either aligned with God or against him. And as separate beings, they demonstrate one of the two natures within humanity.

The parable of the prodigal and his brother reveals the same from a more comprehensive and deeper spiritual perspective. As the son of man, the elder son in the parable exhibits a jealous and righteous ego nature. The younger son depicts what became of the son of God within humanity when Adam and Eve rebelled against God.

The parable ends by showing us what happens when the wayward son of God within us reconciles with our heavenly Father. The spiritual son was dead and came back to life; he was lost and then found. Among the many miracles Jesus performed, bringing the dead back to life was one of them. And scriptures, such as Luke 19:10, testify to Jesus' mission: "For the Son of Man came to seek out and to save the lost."

CHAPTER 13

ABOUT JESUS

And the Word became flesh and lived among us.
—John 1:14a

W HEN WE THINK OF JESUS, we rarely stop to think of what it means that he is the Son of God. How is it that he is God's son? Were God and Jesus up in heaven together, and then 2,000 years ago, the one spirit of Jesus came down to be conceived of the Holy Spirit, born of the Virgin Mary as a human being? Many people believe this to be so.

Yes, Jesus is God's son. He was conceived of the Holy Spirit and born of the Virgin Mary as a human being. But if we are all created in the image and likeness of God, and Jesus embodies this same spirit, Jesus cannot be a completely separate entity external to us.

This assertion of Jesus' unity with us may sound confusing to those who believe he was one spirit who came down from heaven 2,000 years ago and is only inside those who decide to follow him. However, we cannot separate

Jesus from God. We can recognize our link to Jesus through humanity in his documented ancestry. And although we typically consider our ancestry only through our bloodline, the genealogy of Jesus may also remind us of our spiritual origin.

The Gospel of Luke 3:23–38 records the genealogy of Jesus, beginning with his father, Joseph, and ending with the first man, Adam. Here are some relevant verses: "He was the son (as was thought) of Joseph son of Heli"; "son of Jacob, son of Isaac, son of Abraham"; "son of Seth, son of Adam, son of God" (vv. 23b, 34, 38).

The "son of Seth, son of Adam, son of God" shows our link to Jesus as a human being in the creation of humanity. However, although we relate to Jesus as a human being, he still stands above all others in a category of his own. The apostle Paul proclaims: "He is the image of the invisible God, the firstborn of all creation" (Col 1:15). Jesus is the perfect original creation, the Son of Man and the Son of God; he is human and divine, two perfect natures in one human being.

The title for Jesus as the "Son of Man" displays his humanity. "The Son of Man has authority on earth to forgive sins" (Mark 2:10) since he is the only one who obeyed God, even unto death. In contrast to the Son of Man, we are a "son of man" (i.e., one among the many).

Jesus' title as the "Son of God" confirms his divinity. The Son of God embodies the fullness of God: "For in him the whole fullness of deity dwells bodily" (Col 2:9). In contrast to the Son of God, we are a "son of God" (i.e., one among the many).

Jesus is also the Word, and the spiritual life that was once the light of all people:

> In the beginning was the Word, and the Word was with God, and the Word was God. He was in the beginning with God. All things came into being through him, and without him not one thing came into being. What has come into being in him was life, and the life was the light of all people.
> —John 1:1–4

The son of God within a human being is like a candle that lost its divine flame when Adam and Eve fell. Jesus, the Son of God, rekindles the candle of those who follow him and submit to his Word: "For as all die in Adam, so all will be made alive in Christ" (1 Cor 15:22).

THE PURPOSE OF THE TREE

The purpose of the tree of knowledge of good and evil was to allow Adam and Eve the opportunity to show their love for God, since love must be chosen rather than forced. Therefore, God had given them the power of free will: "It was he who created humankind in the beginning, and he left them in the power of their own free choice" (Sir 15:14).

The first thing the serpent did when he appeared to Adam and Eve was trick them into doubting God's Word. Then he tempted them with jealousy to choose their ego to rule and abandon their spiritual relationship with God. Had they chosen to love and obey God, they would have gained the power and wisdom to master the temptation of sin. Yet, instead of mastering the temptation of sin, the sons of God became enslaved by it.

BORN FROM ABOVE

In the Gospel of John 3:1–21, a respected Jewish leader named Nicodemus questioned Jesus about his teachings. Nicodemus was a Pharisee who believed in following the Law to the letter and opposed the ministry of Jesus.

Jesus began by emphasizing the importance of being born of the Spirit: "Very truly, I tell you, no one can see the kingdom of God without being born from above" (v. 3). Nicodemus found Jesus' statement to be absurd because he could only comprehend a physical birth.

Then Jesus clarified that the flesh (i.e., the ego nature) and the spiritual are two distinct entities: "What is born of the flesh is flesh, and what is born of the Spirit is spirit. Do not be astonished that I said to you, you must be born from above" (vv. 6–7).

Jesus further described what happens when someone is born from the Spirit above. They change so suddenly that their friends and family do not understand what has come over them: "The wind blows where it chooses, and you hear the sound of it, but you do not know where it comes from or where it goes. So it is with everyone who is born of the Spirit" (v. 8).

Nicodemus could not grasp the spiritual teachings of Jesus because his ego nature had blinded him entirely. As 1 Corinthians 2:14 explains: "Those who are unspiritual do not receive the gifts of God's Spirit, for they are foolishness to them, and they are unable to understand them because they are spiritually discerned."

TALKING TO JESUS

Some people think of prayer only as a set order of words, which we stop to say to a revered deity; like writing a letter, a prayer consists of some main, formal elements. Prayer has a salutation to God, a few paragraphs of appreciation and praise, then perhaps a petition, followed by an affectionate, complimentary closing.

Respectfully, God genuinely loves to hear and answer our sincere, formal prayers. Yet also, as I learned in early childhood, prayer may be simply conversing with God or Jesus. I talk to Jesus often, like a close friend and confidant. Even when making a minor decision, I might say, "What do you think, Jesus? What should I do?"

For example, once, I could not decide which of the two routes I should take on my way home. Either way, I would enjoy the drive. So, I asked, "What do you think, Jesus? Which way should I go this time?" I had to choose quickly, so I exited the interstate and took the longer way. Less than five minutes later, an announcement came over the radio that a fatal accident had just occurred on the route I did not take.

My most incredible experience of asking Jesus for guidance was when he helped me with some trees in my yard. Two massive hackberry trees were a nuisance, attracting bugs, releasing pollen all over my sun porch and car, and blocking the morning sunlight. They were in a steep embankment, just beyond the small, level backyard area, and a large branch of the one was touching my sun porch roof.

After getting many estimates from local tree removal services, I grew discouraged. They were either well over my budget, untrustworthy, uninsured or lacked the required heavy machinery. Some suggested removing only the tree closest to the sun porch to reduce the cost, or cutting the trees but not hauling them away.

After two months, I slumped down on my couch one day and cried out, "Oh Jesus, *please,* you just *gotta* help me with the trees! I don't know what to do, and there's no one left to call."

The next day, while browsing the internet for something unrelated, a picture of a tree removal business appeared in the sidebar. I had called this company when I first started looking for estimates, but I assumed it was no longer operating because the phone number was out of service. It seemed to still be in business, so I sent a message to the owner to ask. He replied immediately and explained he had a temporary technical problem with his phone service when I had previously called his number.

He arrived at my home within 30 minutes. And as I shook his hand to greet him, he said, "Hello, I'm Heh soos' [the Spanish pronunciation of Jesus] to help you with the trees."

Amazing! Jesus sent Jesus to help me with the trees the day after I asked. The cost was well within my budget, and he met all my requirements. Jesus of the tree removal business, and Jesus our Lord, surpassed my expectations in every way.

Jesus, the Wonderful Counselor, answers my calls for help and guides my decisions. Knowing he is always there for me keeps me at peace and assures me that no matter what happens, everything will be okay.

Our self-talk is the constant dialog we have with ourselves throughout the day. By making Jesus part of it, we feel his presence. Even those who do not feel connected to Jesus may sense his presence when they include him in their daily self-talk.

THE RETURN OF JESUS

Many people believe we will all look up to the sky one day and see Jesus riding on a white horse through the clouds of heaven in power and great glory. He will end all sorrows and bring us peace on earth.

By all the signs, it looks like the second coming of Jesus Christ is very near. All the wars, famines, floods, hurricanes, earthquakes, pestilence—and the great, divine awakening happening on the planet today.

The fulfillment of God's prophecy is imminent, but there has always been speculation about how and when Jesus will return. Some believe the return of Jesus Christ will only occur in a limited three-dimensional reality, which we will only view as an external, historical event.

The most surprising belief, exhibiting a historical understanding of Jesus' return, came from an acquaintance of mine. She was excited because her pastor said Jesus would return very soon, and this world-historic event would occur in Jerusalem. Although she could not afford the plane ticket to be there on site, she hoped reporters would go to film Jesus so she could watch his second coming on the television news.

How do you envision the second coming of Jesus? My acquaintance believes we might only witness this in the physical realm, from one location in the world. According to another view, Jesus may manifest to us depending on the state and level of our spirituality. A combination of the two ways is also conceivable.

Now, if the return of the Lord Jesus Christ—the most exciting, extraordinary, prophetic event in human history—is limited to television watching, I would be utterly disenchanted. What if reporters do not get to Jerusalem in time to film it? Or, what if an electrical outage occurs because of the high seismic activity of the event? Many people do not even have televisions. I do not think the Lord will restrict this spectacular event to viewing on our manufactured devices, which all the world is to see.

And I do not expect world peace might suddenly arrive on that day, as in peace for all. Would Jesus drop large "peace packages" like pizza deliveries from drones, first to diffuse wars in the Middle East and then minor conflicts in our backyards?

I believe Jesus will appear historically in Jerusalem, yet also to us supernaturally, wherever we are, before our physical eyes and according to our hearts. Spirit to spirit, and according to the scripture: "Look! He is coming with the clouds; every eye will see him, even those who pierced him" (Rev 1:7).

Peace in our hearts must come first before peace on earth can ever be. After all, the world did not recognize him when he came the first time, so why would God send another Jesus to those who do not recognize the one who is already here?

> He was in the world, and the world came into being through him; yet the world did not know him.
> —John 1:10

PART II

A STORY
OF
FORGIVENESS

Chapter 14

About Daddy

This is the story about Daddy.

DADDY'S FIRST NAME was Joseph, but friends and family called him "Jimmy" since his middle name was James. He was born on March 7, 1931, and died on February 18, 2002.

He and Mama raised my ten siblings and me in the suburbs of Buffalo, New York. In birth order, there were two boys, seven girls, and two more boys. I am the seventh child and the fifth girl.

Daddy was a hardworking man and a carpenter by trade. He only had an elementary school education and, later, a GED diploma, but he was very intelligent.

He loved making children's toys and other wooden crafts. I have always admired his unique artistic abilities, evident in his beautiful handwriting.

Though Daddy needed to be frugal while supporting a large family, his comments about his Depression-era childhood sounded like a broken record. He often emphasized how good things were for me while growing up, compared to his youth. He once asked to borrow the pin from my pants, and it surprised him I did not have one. As a boy, he had always had a pin because his mother bought his pants two sizes too big so he could grow into them.

Daddy was beyond meticulous. The man paid attention to every little detail and rarely missed a trick. Sometimes, he inspected our work after we had finished our housecleaning chores. We always checked everything carefully. Heaven help us if we missed any dust balls on the floors or in the corners of the rooms.

Daddy was very strict and sometimes capricious, too. The ways he taught respect were very odd. He blew up if you broke his rule, requiring you never to refer to either parent using the indefinite pronoun. And, "You should always fear God, and you should always fear your father," he would say. When I was eight, he explained "fear" was another word for love and respect, but I did not understand. I loved and respected Daddy, but I was afraid of him.

And he sternly forbade us from running in the house. Whenever he caught me running on the wooden bedroom stairs, I had to write the sentence, "I must not run up the stairs or down the stairs in the house," 100 times. When I gave him my finished paper, he would inspect my penmanship and then ask if I learned my lesson.

Sometimes people—even Mama—called Daddy a "stubborn German" or an "old Kraut" because of his headstrong manner. You could not tell him anything without provoking an opposing view.

A BUTTERFLY OR INK

I always thought Daddy saw things differently from most people. I will never forget when I was four, and he got very upset about a bath towel.

All our family bath towels were very plain and worn thin, except for the large, thick, bright white one that Daddy always used for his bath. The prettiest towel in the house, his special towel was multicolored, decorated all over with cheerful flowers in red, orange, and yellow. And in the center was one pretty blue butterfly.

One night, Daddy came storming out of the bathroom and charging through the house. "Who got blue ink on this towel? It's the best towel in the house and the only one big enough for me. Now, somebody has *ruined* it with ink!"

Mama and my older siblings all tried to tell him the blue ink was, in fact, a butterfly, yet Daddy remained unconvinced. Everyone else saw a pretty blue butterfly, and only Daddy saw a damaging blot of blue ink.

THE SAINT JOSEPH SUNDAY MISSAL

We were a devout Roman Catholic family. My siblings and I went to the Catholic grammar school in our parish, and our family faithfully attended Sunday Mass.

We always filled up a whole pew in church. And my older sisters usually pushed me into the pew first, after Daddy, so I would be the one to sit by him.

It wasn't that I thought Daddy had the cooties. It was just that Mama always sat on the side of his good ear, and he was almost deaf in the other. Whoever sat by Daddy had to say the prayers and sing loud enough for him to hear during Mass. If he could not hear them, that person would have to write the day's reading from his Saint Joseph Sunday Missal when we got home.

My prayers and singing were usually too weak for Daddy to hear. So, I often wrote out those Sunday readings from his thick, black Sunday Missal. (And come to think of it, I do not believe my siblings *ever* did.)

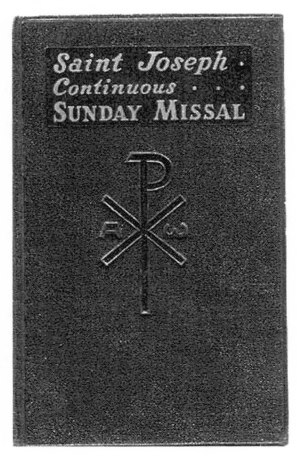

While everyone else was playing outside on sunny Sunday afternoons, I was writing at the kitchen table for about two hours. Then, after Daddy knew I had had enough of it, he would stand me in front of him and talk to me. He would ask what I had learned at Mass and from my written words. Then, he would discuss my handwriting, too.

THE FIRST COMMUNION PRAYER BOOK

Then once, after I finished writing some of Daddy's Saint Joseph Sunday Missal, it occurred to him to ask me about my prayer book. He said I should have received a prayer book when I made my First Communion the month before. Since I did not have one, Daddy brought me a little First Communion prayer book he received when he was seven. He made me promise I would take good care of this prayer book because it was very special to him.

This gift from my father was very special to me, too, since Daddy rarely gave me affection and individual attention. I treasured his little First Communion prayer book, full of colorful pictures of heavenly angels and children's prayers. I read it night after night, under the covers in bed, with a flashlight. And when I recited the prayers, I always prayed for Daddy.

I read it so much that the prayer book eventually fell apart. Then, Daddy got upset with me for not taking better care of it. He reminded me of my lapse for a long time afterward.

Years.

NOT BORED

I had to be careful in my childhood about what I said when Daddy was around. One time when I was eight, he heard me say I was bored. What a *terrible* mistake!

His eyebrows went up, and his jaw dropped. *"Bored!* You should *never* be bored! That is a waste of *life!* Do you really get *bored?* Something is *wrong* with a person who gets bored! I need to get you something to do—*quick!"* Within minutes, I was painting the walls of Daddy's workshop. I assure you, the job was extremely boring.

Occasionally after that, Daddy would say I *looked* bored. I would quickly change my facial expression while thinking up any conceivable thing I was about to do. His tactics worked because I had never been bored a single day since.

Because of Daddy's peculiar ways, I was timid as a child around him. Whenever he tried to get me to open up and talk to him, I gave him the answers I thought he wanted to hear. And it was difficult for me to look him in the eye.

A TEENAGE EFFORT

In a silent effort to become closer to Daddy, I took a woodworking class in 10th grade. Excited about the class, he prepared some lessons to teach me his expertise.

But I was just a kid. Soon, I ran off to be with my friends instead of showing up for the lessons. I swore he had planned them for Friday nights just to keep me from having a social life.

Then Daddy wrote me a sincere letter asking why I stopped coming to the lessons. He even assured me he would understand if I changed my mind. I was too afraid to answer for fear of disappointing him.

LEAVING HOME

When I was 17, I ran away from home. I know Daddy loved our family sincerely, but his dark side made things difficult. He had a terrible temper, especially when he drank. You never knew when he would fly off the handle or for what. Sometimes police or social workers came to our door because of the uproar.

I wanted freedom from Daddy's strict rules and brutal, physical abuse directed at teenage girls. One by one, my older sisters had all left home at about the same age. And Nancy, my next-younger sister, had run away the week before and was not coming back. I felt alone.

My parents' marriage was in its darkest hour, too. The handwriting was on the wall that Mama would soon leave Daddy. I thought it would be easier on her if I left anyhow. She would have just my three youngest siblings to take with her then.

Though, no matter what Daddy was like all those years, my heart was very heavy. It felt strange—sad and surreal—knowing he and Mama were really splitting up. Divorce, the death of my parents' marriage, was in progress now, and I could not bear to stay to watch.

Once upon a time, we had been a big family, living in a five-bedroom house full of kids of all ages. Somewhere music would be playing, the television blasting, and the kitchen telephone ringing off the wall. Every day, the faint sounds of buzzing saws and the smell of warm sawdust drifted across the backyard from Daddy's workshop. And every day at 5:00 pm, like clockwork, we all sat down together and said a prayer before our family dinner.

Then, suddenly, I was the oldest sibling living at home, and the house was dark and nearly empty. The music had stopped; the television was off; the telephone had stopped ringing, and Daddy's workshop was still. Our prayers and family dinners faded into forgotten memories of the past.

I was very scared. Things were much worse than ever before. Day after day, I stayed quietly in my bedroom, where the only sounds I heard were of Mama and Daddy fighting, which shook the house. Daddy was out of control, drinking and badly abusing Mama.

My parents never spoke against each other openly, and I could not talk to Mama about what was happening because she never discussed her problems with me. "Marriage problems" was a silent subject, none of my business, and awkward to bring up. I was afraid to leave Mama in a dangerous situation, but I did not know how to help her, and I knew my older brothers would come to her aid. I saw no recourse but to stay out of the way. So, I left.

CHAPTER 15

A ROSE FOR DADDY

Husbands should love their wives as they do their
own bodies. He who loves his wife loves
himself.
—Eph 5:28

BY THE EARLY 1980s, I was married with four small
children and living in Houston, Texas. Then, one day
in the summer of 1985, Daddy called and said he was living
in Waco, Texas. He wanted to come for a brief visit and
introduce me to his new wife, Rose.

I was pleased to hear from him. I missed having him
in my life since I had not seen him in over ten years—since
I left home. So, he and Rose came to Houston, and we had
a pleasant afternoon visit.

Rose was a lovely, petite, red-haired Italian woman
with a bubbly personality. She and Daddy seemed crazy
about each other. Before they got married, they dated for
eighteen months. They eagerly told me about their love
story, how they found each other, and all the little things

they had in common. They said it felt like they had known each other a long time when they first met.

Then Daddy announced Rose was the first woman he had ever known who owned a gun. Rose then became emotional, insisting she needed a gun to protect herself from her first husband.

Then I choked on my beverage right in front of them, and spilled it down my blouse, when Rose said she had divorced her husband because he was an alcoholic and had been abusive. Her ex-husband sounded exactly like her new husband, Daddy, sitting with his arm around her across the table from me.

Rose shook her head and looked at me. "You know, Donna, you just can't live with someone like that. I was afraid he would kill me, and he almost did a few times."

The similarity was eerie. Mama could have been sitting there, saying those words. I wanted Daddy to be happy and Rose, too. Yet, I worried for Rose and desired her safety. I could only hope Daddy had changed.

The following year, Rose divorced Daddy. He never remarried after that.

Chapter 16

Our Waco Visit

If anyone is in Christ, there is a new creation:
everything old has passed away; see, everything
has become new!
—2 Cor 5:17

AFTER HIS DIVORCE from Rose, Daddy invited me to
visit him in Waco one day. He was excited to report he
began following Jesus recently and had a spiritual
conversion. I was eager to see him for a three-day weekend.

I found Daddy living in a somewhat blighted
neighborhood, in a little house needing repairs. The
strange layout of the house consisted of tiny rooms with
gloomy, paneled walls, mismatched furniture, and missing
kitchen cabinets. Daddy said the house embarrassed him,
especially because he was a carpenter. He could not
remodel it since the cost of divorcing Rose had depleted his
bank account.

Despite his hardships, Daddy was bursting with joy
and enthusiasm for Jesus that entire weekend. He had

become a completely different man from the one I had known him to be.

On the first night of our visit, he anxiously ran to get his Holy Bible. Then he pulled up a metal chair before me and sat down. "Oh! I've been waiting for this! I want you to teach me *all about Jesus* while you're here! You know all about him—I *know* you do!"

So, each night, Daddy and I talked until the wee hours of the morning, and I taught him what I knew about Jesus, at the time. I retold some biblical stories about Jesus and how they related to my life.

JESUS WALKS ON THE WATER

Daddy's favorite story was in the Gospel of John 6, when Jesus walked on the water and delivered his disciples out of a perilous situation and safely to shore. This passage is an allegory of Jesus spiritually saving us:

> When evening came, his disciples went down to the sea, got into a boat, and started across the sea to Capernaum. It was now dark, and Jesus had not yet come to them. The sea became rough because a strong wind was blowing. When they had rowed about three or four miles, they saw Jesus walking on the sea and coming near the boat, and they were terrified. But he said to them, "It is I; do not be afraid." Then they wanted to take him into the boat, and immediately the boat reached the land toward which they were going.
> —John 6:16–21

I see myself as a disciple on the boat, and the boat symbolizes my life. I was once like a lost passenger in the dark, on a boat with no captain. The strong winds and rough waves were my life's problems, tossing me about on the sea of life. Instead of controlling my life, life was controlling me. And, like the disciples, I, too, experienced fear—in a mystical sense—when I unmistakably felt Jesus approaching me. In the summer of 1978, signs of Jesus appeared everywhere.

One day, something drew my attention to the meaning of "BC" and "AD." The recorded years before the birth of Jesus are BC, "Before Christ." And the years after his birth are AD, for the Latin phrase "Anno Domini." Anno Domini translates to "in the year of our Lord." Every year since the birth of Jesus is another year of our Lord because he is still alive today. The world measures time according to the birth of Jesus Christ, the most powerful man who ever walked the earth.

Then the Sunday Houston Chronicle came, with a large article about a group of scientists who went to Italy for a forensic examination of the Shroud of Turin, the burial cloth of Jesus. Their expedition concluded that the photographic imprint of a bearded man, bearing the wounds of a Roman-style crucifixion, on a blood-stained cloth, remained a mystery. The newspaper article so captivated me that I bought the book, *The Shroud of Turin,* by Ian Wilson. Fascinating plates in the book showed burn marks caused by a high burst of energy imprinted on the linen cloth when Jesus resurrected.

And then, one day, a stranger handed me a brochure about heaven that began with the words, "You do not even know what tomorrow will bring" (Jas 4:14a). This got me thinking about insurance. Even though I had a variety of insurance policies—life, health, property, and vehicle—I could have died the next day, and I had no insurance for my *eternal life*.

Signs of Jesus kept swirling around me that entire summer. Then, like the disciples, I immediately "arrived upon land" when I received him into my "boat" (i.e., my life) and asked him to live in my heart. Anchored to the rock of salvation then, I knew where I stood spiritually and where I was going.

ROLL AWAY THE STONE

Daddy and I turned to the Gospel of John 11:1–44 to discuss when Jesus raised Lazarus from the dead. The story is an allegory of Jesus bringing our spirit back to life.

Lazarus and his two sisters, Mary and Martha, were in Jesus' close inner circle of friends. When the sisters sent a message to Jesus that their brother was ill, everyone wondered why he did not immediately go to heal Lazarus then. Instead, he delayed and went to his tomb four days after Lazarus died.

Seeing his friends and many others weeping over Lazarus' death moved Jesus deeply. He began to weep when he found everyone in such sadness. Then, when he came to the tomb: "It was a cave, and a stone was lying against it. Jesus said, 'Take away the stone'" (vv. 38b–39a).

Now, if Jesus could raise Lazarus from the dead, he could have also moved the enormous stone that blocked the cave entrance for the people, but he did not. Instead, he placed the responsibility on the *people;* they had to do their part before Jesus could do his. Our ego nature is like a heavy stone that blocks our hearts. We must do our part and remove the resistance from our ego nature before Jesus can bring our divine spirit back to life.

After they rolled away the stone, Jesus said a prayer for the sake of the crowd. And then: "He cried with a loud voice, 'Lazarus, come out!' The dead man came out, his hands and feet bound with strips of cloth, and his face wrapped in a cloth. Jesus said to them, 'Unbind him, and let him go'" (vv. 43–44).

Lazarus rising from the dead and returning to life when Jesus called him symbolizes Jesus restoring our deadened spirit to its divine nature when he calls us; the command to remove Lazarus' burial garments means that Jesus liberates us from the bondage of our ego nature.

The ego that rules our lives will naturally oppose the Spirit. For eternal life in heaven, we must be in our divine spiritual nature; hence, we must wholeheartedly conquer any opposition.

I had to roll away that stone before becoming a Christian. (When I confess to others that I was initially hesitant, some people respond with, *"Oh, Donna!"* as if they had not been? I believe most go through a period of reflection, as Jesus calls them and gradually opens their spiritual eyes.) My ego invented some excuses at first, but then, every time, God prevailed with undisputable truth:

I worried God would expect constant perfection. What if I failed and could not live up to such holy Christian standards? I was just an ordinary, young, stay-at-home wife and mother with no serious habits I would have to surrender, but I am far from perfect.

But (the truth is), a Christian does not experience judgment from God. Jesus verified this: "Anyone who hears my word and believes him who sent me has eternal life, and does not come under judgment, but has passed from death to life" (John 5:24). In fact, Jesus even said it is the other way around: "The one who rejects me and does not receive my word has a judge; on the last day the word that I have spoken will serve as judge" (John 12:48).

God also understands that as long as we walk the earth, our shadowy ego nature will tempt us. He promises to help us in those times: "No testing has overtaken you that is not common to everyone. God is faithful, and he will not let you be tested beyond your strength, but with the testing he will also provide the way out so that you may be able to endure it" (1 Cor 10:13).

I figured I would have to become religious by making this commitment, which implied living a restricted and boring life. I did not know all the "dos and don'ts" of Christian religions. And which is the right one, anyhow?

But (the truth is), religion and spirituality are not the same. Living in our spiritual nature by simply following Jesus differs from being religious, which entails holding onto a particular foundational set of beliefs and rituals.

And while there are essential distinctions between Christian denominations, the core beliefs outweigh the differences. The core beliefs that form the bedrock of the Christian faith are: there is only one God, eternally existing as the Father, Son, and Holy Spirit; Jesus Christ is Lord and Savior; and the sacred text of Christianity is the Holy Bible.

Some Christians impressed me as very judgmental, though, and I did not want to associate with such people. I had been a first-time visitor to some cliquish Christian churches where, after the service, even the pastor only nodded at me or hurriedly shook my hand to greet a familiar church member behind me. Jesus would not treat others like that.

But (the truth is), Christians do not follow other people; they follow Jesus. I should base my decision for my eternal life on the teachings of Jesus, not on the attitudes or actions of others.

My family puts me down a lot. They will call me a "Jesus freak" or "holy roller" or accuse me of joining a cult.

But (the truth is), I need to heed what Jesus said about this: "Everyone therefore who acknowledges me before others, I also will acknowledge before my Father in heaven; but whoever denies me before others, I also will deny before my Father in heaven" (Matt 10:32–33).

Then my ego suggested I should "think about it for a while. This is a big, life-changing decision."

But (the truth is), isn't doing nothing or putting it off the same as saying no? And what sense is there in waiting, rejecting God's love, and missing the chance of a better life now and eternal life in heaven?

After I rolled away the stone and committed to following Jesus, I discovered that there is no greater love than God's love. And a new life in the Spirit is like having a new pair of eyes. Seeing the world from both sides, the spiritual and the ego, has given me much insight and has enriched my life immensely. And since then, I have met many genuine Christians and visited many Spirit-filled churches with friendly people who have welcomed me.

Just as Jesus called Lazarus to awaken from the dead, Ephesians 5:14 also calls us: "Sleeper, awake! Rise from the dead, and Christ will shine on you."

TWO KINDS OF BREAD

When Daddy asked about prayer during our visit, the significance of the Last Supper, recorded in the Gospel of Mark 14:12–15, came to mind. The Last Supper occurred on the first day of the Feast of Unleavened Bread. Jesus ate his last meal of unleavened bread with the twelve apostles in a large upper room of a house.

The upper room represents our higher spiritual self. Unleavened bread, made without yeast, symbolizes the humble spiritual nature, and bread with yeast is the puffed-up ego. Apostle Paul implies the two kinds of bread represent our two natures: "Your boasting is not a good thing. Do you not know that a little yeast leavens the whole batch of dough? Clean out the old yeast so that you may be a new batch, as you really are unleavened" (1 Cor 5:6–7a).

We must communicate with God from spirit to Spirit, not ego to Spirit. Jesus confirmed this in John 4:24: "God is spirit, and those who worship him must worship in spirit and truth." So, when we pray, we humbly go to our "upper room" to commune with Jesus in spirit to Spirit, without a puffed-up ego. Worship services use unleavened wafers for Holy Communion for this reason.

A LIGHT BORN IN THE DARK

Above all, I wanted to share the story of the miraculous birth of Jesus with Daddy, the most amazing miracle of all. The Gospel of Luke 2:1–7 recounts the historical world event in just a few scant verses, but many miss its profound symbolic significance.

Mary and Joseph were in Bethlehem to pay their taxes, and when the time came for the birth of Jesus to be born in a barn: "She gave birth to her firstborn son and wrapped him in bands of cloth, and laid him in a manger, because there was no place for them in the inn" (v. 7).

The nativity scenes during the Christmas season beautifully capture the above verse in a cozy barn setting. However, a realistic view of the event and circumstances shows Mary and Joseph were of little significance to the world then. As unknowns in society, they could not get a warm room at the inn for their child's birth.

The prestigious inn with no vacancies symbolizes the pompous world full of outward appearances and things—the most unlikely place for the birth of Jesus. Jesus was born in a poor barn, and his parents wrapped him in rags to keep him warm. Then they placed him in a manger, an animal's feeding trough on a dirt floor, as a makeshift newborn crib. The birth of Jesus in a lowly barn represents his spiritual birth in the most humble part of our hearts.

In the summer of 1978, I was a naïve and adventurous 21-year-old when my husband and I moved to Houston, Texas, for his new job. Until then, we had been living in Knoxville, Tennessee, for several years. Since I had never been to Houston, I learned about the city from my husband and the newspapers. Houston, Texas, sounded exciting, and definitely, the place to be. So, my husband secured a rental house on the outskirts of Houston, and then we moved our family to the great city. I could not *wait* to get there!

On the day we arrived, we stopped at the large neighborhood grocery store before going to the house. I stayed in the car with our small children while my husband went into the store for a few items. It was mid-afternoon. Within minutes, I started melting from the intense heat of the sun. The Houston sun seemed much closer to earth than the sun I left behind in Tennessee.

As I waited for my husband, I surveyed my surroundings. I was in a vast, unpaved, dusty parking lot with cars everywhere and swarms of chattering people from what looked like every nation on the planet. There was nothing but dust, cars, strangers, and the big scorching sun hovering right above the hood of the car. Such drastically foreign surroundings were like a loud slap on my face. I did not know Houston could be such a dreadful place. *I think I just landed right in hell!*

When we arrived at our new house, and I opened the door, a cockroach scurried across the kitchen countertop. I had never seen a cockroach before then in my life. And every night after that, gigantic cockroaches overtook our outdoor patio.

Such unpleasant details of daily life had never entered my mind when I dreamed of our great adventure. I secretly wondered why I had agreed to such a drastic move, but I could not admit my regret when my husband asked if I wanted to turn back. Since we had been through a lot to get to hell, I felt committed to staying there.

I spent my summer days in isolation from all ordinary channels of contact with the outside world. My husband's new job required six- and seven-day double shifts, and I did not have a driver's license then. I was housebound with a two-year-old and nine-month-old twins. The internet was nonexistent, long-distance calls were expensive in those days, and I was 1,400 miles away from my big family in the north.

So there I was, living in a sweltering hot, buggy place where I did not know a soul. I was the picture of an unknown in society, in a meager barn within a foreign city on a cold (i.e., lonely) night.

My only source of entertainment was watching television late at night. I preferred movies, but only one Christian television ministry was available. I believe my soul took the path to Houston, so I would hear Jesus calling me in this way, and I would answer him. I had to be alone for this to happen.

Now, I had always thought of myself as a Christian. I even had a very moving, spiritual experience when I became a Christian at seven (although I had gradually drifted into a quiescent state over the years). But I had always lived a reasonably decent life by sound Christian principles; I treated others as I would want others to treat me; I did not purposefully hurt anyone. I am a nice person.

However, the woman on the television ministry seemed to be a different kind of Christian from me; she was bubbling with unusual joy and enthusiasm for Jesus. Admittedly, I was not as excited about Jesus as she was. Night after night, I listened to her stories, sometimes through tears of joy rolling down her cheeks, about the wonderful things Jesus had done for her recently. And she often repeated things like, "Turn to Jesus, and he will do such things for you too."

I did not understand what made her like that. What was I missing? In my analytical mind, I tried to figure it out as if there were a complicated process to know Jesus as well as she did.

She also repeatedly insisted I pray to Jesus, ask forgiveness for my sins, and invite him into my heart. I figured there must be more to it than that, though; I was waiting for her to lay out the rest of the plan and tell me what else I would need to do.

But the more the woman said it, the more I heard it, and she was gradually awakening me from the deafness of my ego nature. Then, one night, I reached an epiphany: to come to know Jesus as she did was as simple as saying the heartfelt prayer she kept advising. It was *so simple* that I kept missing it.

So, alone and away from the pompous world full of people, outward appearances, and things, I knelt in front of the television in my little living room and said a prayer to Jesus. At that very moment, I experienced an indescribable miracle—a burden lifted, a sudden inner peace, and unspeakable joy that brought me to tears. My heart became a living manger for Jesus that night, when the greatest of kings, in my humble surroundings, gave birth to his light in the dark.

THE WOMAN AT THE WELL

When I awoke the next morning, I was so ecstatic that I wanted to tell the whole world about Jesus, just like the woman on the television ministry did. And, like the Samaritan woman at the well, in the Gospel of John 4:1–42.

The Samaritan woman went to the well to fill her water jar and met Jesus there. In their conversation, Jesus declared: "Those who drink of the water that I will give them will never be thirsty. The water that I will give will become in them a spring of water gushing up to eternal life" (v. 14). When the woman discovered he was the Messiah, she was so astonished that she dropped her water jar and ran to the city to tell everyone she had met Jesus: "Then the woman left her water jar and went back to the city. She said to the people, 'Come and see a man who told me everything I have ever done! He cannot be the Messiah, can he?'" (vv. 28–29).

The Samaritan woman at the well illustrates many Christians today. We are just as excited to tell others about Jesus as that woman was, 2,000 years ago.

Then, unusual things happened in the following days. I wanted to get a Holy Bible right away, but money was tight because of the moving and relocation expenses. Within a few days, an unexpected check came in the mail from my husband's past employer of years before. How did they find our address? It was just enough to buy three Bibles—one for me, one for my little daughter, and one for our family.

I suddenly wanted to attend church, too. And two people knocked on my door shortly after and invited me to their church. They even sent bus transportation. By God's grace, answers came to me of their own accord concerning many things.

Soon afterward, my time in Houston improved. My husband got a better job, we bought a house, I got my driver's license, and I made new friends. We remained in Houston for nine years.

PERSONAL EXPERIENCES

Once we learn the truth about something, it convicts us; we cannot undo what we know. The birth of Jesus Christ within our hearts transforms us, and our spiritual desires start replacing our ego-driven ones. Such a shift in attitude has a substantial impact on our lives.

The circumstances that lead us to Jesus and what follows are unique to each person. Some new Christians may feel powerful emotions in their new birth experience, while others may initially question theirs. However, we base our new birth on trust in Jesus, not emotions; we cannot trust our feelings because they can act like rollercoasters and are affected by outside forces. Assuredly, new Christians soon become confident in their new birth, if not immediately. I have never met anyone who invited Jesus into their heart, stayed on course, and then stated, "I tried that, and it made no difference." Jesus is true to his promise if we are, and he never rejects anyone. He will be born in the heart of anyone who believes in him and asks.

And Christians, like everyone else, face difficulties; their lives are not suddenly perfect or happily ever after. But because of their new relationship with God through Jesus Christ, they gain wisdom to deal with life's problems righteously, according to spiritual principles, and no longer doubt God hears their prayers.

New Christians often inquire about their next steps after their spiritual conversion. Finding other Christians in the community and a Spirit-filled church is essential for encouragement, support, and friendships. If this is not possible, many wonderful Christian ministries are online.

Becoming a strong and mature Christian also requires reading the Bible. Reading the Bible strengthens our faith, helps us to grow spiritually, and keeps us from going astray. Although some people find the Bible intimidating, many versions available today are easy to understand. The New Testament, which contains Jesus' teachings and marks the beginning of early Christianity, is a good place to start.

SPIRITUAL MIRACLES TODAY

Many of Jesus' miracles serve as allegories of our spiritual transformation. The Holy Bible is a timeless book, and when we understand how its stories relate to us today, we realize the miracles of Jesus are of great importance to our spiritual growth.

Jesus saves us, lost passengers, from our sinking ships like he rescued his disciples from the turbulent sea. He heals us of our blind and deaf egos like he healed the physically blind and deaf during his ministry on earth. He brings our spirits back to life when we roll away the stones that block our hearts. And when we are alone and in the dark, we may ask Jesus to be born in our hearts: "A new heart I will give you, and a new spirit I will put within you; and I will remove from your body the heart of stone and give you a heart of flesh" (Ezek 36:26).

THE LITTLE WOODEN PLAQUE

Daddy was overflowing with generosity throughout our weekend visit. He gave me some of his various kitchen gadgets, mismatched furniture, and an assortment of household items. It was even comical. Whenever he entered a room, he would find something to pick up. "Here, do you want this? I never use this. You have it—I insist! Go on, take it, *take* it!"

Most of all, I have always treasured the little wooden plaque Daddy gave me that weekend. He was very proud that it was one of his creations. He pointed to it across the living room on his television and asked excitedly, "Donna! Donna! What do you see?"

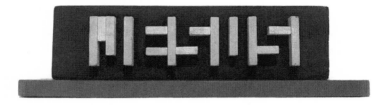

I had to stare at it for a moment before I realized what it said. Then, with a song in his voice, he laughed. "You gotta keep *looking,* Donna, until you see *Jesus!*"

If Wishes Were Horses

At the end of the third night of our Waco visit, Daddy said with unusual utmost passion, "Oh, I wish I had a way to tell others about Jesus like you do!"

Then his jaw dropped, and his eyes got big and glassy. He stared straight ahead. "Oh! Can you imagine if together we could come up with a way to tell the whole world about Jesus? Wouldn't that be fun? Oh, how I would love to do that with you someday!"

He slowly turned to me. "C'mon, Donna! You've always been good at stuff like this. You're creative! You can think of *some* way, can't you?" He slapped his leg. "What can we do to make that happen?"

"Yeah, that would be fun... I guess... ?"

I had a blank look on my face. Daddy's request was a mighty tall order. I have a great imagination, but I could see no way of ever granting his far-fetched wish back then.

My response discouraged him. "Yeah, I know. If wishes were horses, then beggars would ride 'em, right?"

"Huh?"

"Oh, maybe you're too young to know that one. It's an old saying that means, 'What are the chances?' or 'Maybe in a million years.' Think about it—if wishes were horses, then beggars like me would want to ride 'em, right?"

He looked around his living room and laughed. "Hah! Look at me, sitting here in my little cracker box in Waco, Texas. I'm just a poor ol' beggar. How could someone like me ever get the chance to tell the whole world about Jesus? And what can I ever do for Jesus, anyhow? Jesus doesn't need me... but it sure would be fun, Donna, if you and I could ever do that someday." Then he shrugged. "Oh, well... I've always been a dreamer, so I can dream it 'til then, right?"

CHAPTER 17

FRONT PORCH STORIES

Where two or three are gathered in my name, I am
there among them.
—Matt 18:20

IN THE LATE 1980s, my family and I moved back to
Tennessee. We bought a big, old Victorian house in a
small town outside of Knoxville.

After we settled in, I invited Daddy to come and live
with us, and he did. Although we did not maintain a close
relationship over those years, we had been on good terms
since our Waco visit.

We began spending hours visiting on the front porch
together as soon as he arrived. We talked about anything at
all that came to mind. Now was our chance to catch up for
all time and connect in a way we never had before. In my
entire lifetime, there were very few times, other than our
Waco visit, that I ever had one-on-one visits with Daddy
like those on the front porch in Tennessee.

IMAGINE

During our first visit, I could see Daddy wanted a closer relationship also when he asked, "Do you know what my favorite song is of all time?" Then, in crackled tones, he belted out, "Imagine there's no heaven, It's easy if you try, No hell below us, Above us only sky... Imagine all the people, Living life in peace... Yooouu... You may say I'm a dreamer, But I'm not the only one, I hope someday you'll join us, And the world will live as one."

Then he stood up crookedly, with tears in his eyes, holding out his arms. "Oh, how I love that song! It goes right *through* me every time, and I get goosebumps all over! Imagine what it would be like to have peace on earth like that, Donna, and if we would all be as one? We wouldn't need to go to heaven then, because heaven would be right here on earth. That's what heaven is, right? It's peace on earth. Someday, maybe someday, Donna, we'll have peace on earth. We should always pray for that."

DADDY'S DOOZY

Daddy had a funny sense of humor, though he had usually seemed somber in my childhood and youth. In telling stories, he often gestured with his whole body. If the story had to do with some crazy thing he had done, he introduced the topic by admitting his folly. "Man, I'm a screwball!" Then, standing up and shouting, he would stretch out his arms as an overture to honesty. "Just tell it like it is, right?!"

One day, during a quiet spell on the porch, he looked over at me and rolled his eyes, while sucking on a lifesaver. "Did I ever tell you about how Rose left me to get a divorce?

Man! That was a real *doozy!* You know how I always make sure I unplug everything, and I always lock everything up, tight as a drum, before I go anywhere?"

"Yeah?" Smiling, I sat up in my chair. The story sounded juicy, like something that could only happen to poor ol' Daddy.

"Especially when I lived in *Waco.* I had to have three locks on my front door in that city! I was always afraid of getting *robbed* there."

Now, Daddy was a very "don't-move-my-cheese" kind of guy. Whenever something did not go just right for him or messed up his plans, he pulled out his handkerchief to wipe the sweat off his brow. He did that a *lot.* He also obsessed over safety. It required the patience of Job while he went through all his little rituals, even before he stepped out to the corner store for ten minutes.

And he usually drove some tired, old car at a top speed of about 30 mph. He was a very careful driver to avoid accidents. So careful that if anyone ever got behind "slow Joe" on the road, they would probably try their best to pass him, or pray the old fart would turn off soon.

Daddy explained he and Rose planned to go shopping one day. They had to go to the bank first. But when they were on the front porch, ready to leave, Daddy stopped to go back into the house. He had to check on the coffee pot to be sure he had unplugged it. Meanwhile, Rose got in the car. When Daddy came back out, he carefully locked all three locks on the front door.

"When I turned around, there was Rose, smiling and waving goodbye as she drove away. And there I was, standing on the front porch, *and I had just locked myself out of my own house!* I was so shocked that my jaw hit the floor, and my teeth almost popped right out of my mouth!

"Then once it hit me what had just happened, I panicked. We had $3,500 in our joint checking account, and Rose was heading to the bank all by herself! I ran around to the backyard and broke a kitchen window to get back into the house. I grabbed the keys to the other car and sped off to the bank. I even had to leave the house with a broken window. I never drove so fast in my life!"

There were drive-through lanes on both sides of the bank. Rose was waiting in a lane on one side of the bank while Daddy got into a lane on the other side.

"I was on one side of the bank, trying to take all the money out of our account, while Rose was on the other side, trying to do the same thing. We locked up the bank's computers, and neither of the two tellers could figure out why they could not withdraw the money for either of us. We were both after the same $3,500! When the tellers finally figured out the problem, they had to get the bank manager, who froze our account. Neither of us got any money that day. We both had to wait until we got lawyers.

"I'll never forget how she did that. The gall of it all was that she waited for me to come back out to watch me lock myself out of the house, and so I would see her drive off to the bank by herself."

Daddy laughed hysterically, imitating Rose, waving and smiling as she drove away. "'Goodbye, Jimmy!' Oh, that dirty little you-know-what!"

Then he sat muttering. "I almost had a heart attack that day... I never even saw it coming... and that dumb coffee pot was even unplugged when I went to check it... Oh, why do I always have to be so careful?"

Rose really moved Daddy's cheese that time. Picturing him "speeding" through Waco in his old, tan Chevy Impala and all of that happening to him in about 30 minutes made me laugh until my stomach hurt. (He was just lucky Rose did not use her gun on him.)

After we settled back down, he mused. "But your mother, Donna, no matter how many women I had after her, I never got over her. I made a lot of mistakes, but she was the love of my life. Even to this day."

THE SILENT CONVERSATION

One day while we sat on the porch, I commented that I thought of Daddy as a quiet person. Surprised, he jumped straight up from his chair. "*Quiet?!* Donna, I'm not quiet at *all!* Where did you even *get* that from?"

I knew he was right. The truth was, I had always been the quiet one in our relationship. My remark, which came from my subconscious, told of the barrier I had always felt between us. Like some nameless, dark, unspeakable blob, that barrier was always there.

Daddy stared at me for a moment as if he might cry and shook his head. "You know, Donna, I don't think you ever really knew me... you really didn't... you didn't...."

I felt awkward and sad. I could not look him in the eye, so I looked across the street.

THE LADY IN HIS NEIGHBORHOOD

One day, out of the blue, Daddy told me a different kind of story on the porch, about a lady he knew when he was seven. A pretty lady in his neighborhood always wore a lovely dress, a flower on her lapel, a fine hat, and shiny, high-heeled shoes. Daddy always looked forward to seeing her because she was so polite and friendly. Although he was just a boy, she always stopped to talk with him whenever they met up.

Then, one day, as he was walking down the main street in their neighborhood, the lady came stumbling out of the corner bar, very drunk. "She looked completely disheveled," he said. "Her hat was lopsided, the flower on her lapel was turned out of place, and her shoes were all sloppy and barely still on her feet. She could hardly walk. In that very moment, my *whole image* of that lady completely fell."

Daddy turned to me. "Did that ever happen to you, that your image of a person you really loved and looked up to, completely falls in a single instant? Just like that?" He snapped his fingers, hard. "What I saw made such an impact on me; the memory of it always stuck with me. Such a shame. I was just a little seven-year-old boy, and right up to that very moment, I really loved her. But after seeing her, all drunk and such a mess, I could never even talk to her or look her in the eye after that. Whenever I saw her coming down the sidewalk, I pretended I didn't see her. I would turn and put my head down, and rush to get over to the other side of the street."

Then Daddy seemed very bewildered. "Huh! I don't even know what made me think to *tell* you about that lady, Donna! In my entire lifetime, I never told a single soul about her, not even your mother, and I told her *everything*. And now, for some strange reason, I just told *you*. I have no idea *why!*" Then he kept shaking his head and saying quietly to himself, "Why... did I... just *tell* you... that?"

CONCLUSION

The visits with Daddy on my front porch in Tennessee are among my most cherished memories of him. His backward logic and animated gestures always made his comedy-of-errors stories even funnier than he himself could see. And from all the times he openly shared his heartfelt feelings, I gained a deeper understanding of the father I never really knew.

But a few years later, we had a misunderstanding, and he moved out. It was the last time I saw him before he died. Then in 1996, I moved back to New York and bought a house, after I divorced my husband. Daddy eventually moved back there to live in a nursing home, just a few miles down the road from me.

I will always regret not visiting Daddy in the nursing home before he died. It was not that I did not want to, for I loved him very much. I was just afraid he would not want to see me, so I stayed away.

CHAPTER 18

THE PRAYER OF SAINT FRANCIS OF ASSISI

Lord, make me an instrument of your peace.

Where there is hatred, let me sow love;

Where there is injury, pardon;

Where there is doubt, faith;

Where there is despair, hope;

Where there is darkness, light;

And where there is sadness, joy.

O Divine Master, grant that I may not so much seek to be consoled as to console;

To be understood as to understand;

To be loved as to love.

For it is in giving that we receive,

It is in pardoning that we are pardoned,

And it is in dying that we are born to eternal life.

Amen

THE PRAYER of Saint Francis of Assisi has always had a way of deeply touching me. So, in 2005, when it appeared again before me, I printed it out and framed it for the wall in my home office.

Occasionally, I would stop to recite the prayer. Each time, I pondered its special meaning a little deeper. Soon, while sitting on the living room couch, I would hold the prayer in my hands and read it slowly. I wanted to *pray* this prayer from my heart rather than just repeating the words. Then one day, the line, "Where there is injury, pardon," gave me cause for contemplation.

Many say they love this prayer and claim to have forgiven others. But they have not truly done so. True forgiveness is deeper than a quick decision in the mind or a passing thought. Frequently, someone may say they have forgiven a person only later to remember the same offense, over and over again. A grudge is a refusal to forgive. People hold grudges all the time and even seek revenge. Some are proud of their righteous anger.

While contemplating the Prayer of Saint Francis, one day, I asked, "God, how do I know if I have really forgiven someone?" Then from my inner voice, I heard, "Think of *one* person, Donna, just *one* person."

Right away, this message prompted me to think of Daddy. Although I had said I had forgiven him, I sometimes felt hurt over our broken relationship. Is that my subconscious telling me I had not completely forgiven him? How can I know I have truly done so?

I resolved to pray the prayer more often for a while. Whenever I came to the line, "Where there is injury, pardon," I directed the words to Daddy. I stopped to talk to him in the spirit.

Then one day, I asked, "Daddy, where did things go wrong between us, anyhow? How did it all start?" Just then, I felt him at my shoulder, and I remembered.

> The Advocate, the Holy Spirit, whom the Father will send in my name, will teach you everything, and remind you of all that I have said to you.
> —John 14:26

CHAPTER 19

FORTY YEARS EARLIER

Make me to know your ways, O LORD;
  teach me your paths.
  —Psalm 25:4

SPIRITUAL SUBJECTS always fascinated me in my childhood because of early clairvoyant experiences. So, entering second grade at Our Lady of the Sacred Heart School was a thrilling event.

I took words literally then, and habitually pondered their meanings. At seven, the name of my new school sounded like a fine academy where they taught spiritual mysteries. So, I fully expected to learn all about the Sacred Heart of Jesus there.

The Catholic school would be completely different from the neighboring Public School No. 5 I had been attending. Until then, I could only look across the parking lot from my first-grade classroom and daydream about life and learning in that mystical place on the other side.

My older sisters did not sound happy about school starting that crisp September morning, but I could not wait. Before dawn, I was all decked out in my new Catholic uniform: a navy blue jumper with the "OLSH" emblem, a starched white blouse, and a bright red bowtie.

As I walked through the doors of my new school that morning, I beheld the sight of lovely nuns fluttering up and down the corridor. I watched as they hurried about, forming lines of children as they steadily marched in.

The nuns wore long black veils with white linen squares on their foreheads. They looked like tall, graceful birds in their jet-black gowns. Their veils were wings, flowing along behind them as they moved. They were a gentle flock, smiling and softly greeting the new students.

At the end of the second grade, I was to make my First Holy Communion. It would be the most important upcoming event of the school year.

MISS WILLIAMS

Miss Williams, my second-grade teacher, was the greatest teacher I ever had. She resembled a pretty Barbie doll, with long brown hair, a golden tan, and green eyes as big as saucers. On the second day of school, she bent down and whispered, "My name is Donna, too." It was instant love.

Miss Williams was very calm and had a special way with children. She seemed cool for having a sewing class for the girls while the boys were at the gym. I often talked to her privately at her desk. I loved hearing her gentle voice. She always answered my many questions about First Holy

Communion enticingly. "Yes... but you have to be *ready* for it first..."

THE SEVEN SACRAMENTS

One day, Miss Williams announced that our First Holy Communion was one of the seven sacraments of the Roman Catholic Church. We would learn about the other sacraments in a later religion class.

Seven sacraments! Everything about me was seven, which was my lucky number. I was seven, the seventh child, born in the seventh month of 1957. My house number, 417, even had a seven in it. Whatever the seven sacraments were (I had no clue), from the blessed-sounding title, I was in a hurry to make all of them. With a sign-me-up eagerness, I told Miss Williams of my readiness to make all seven sacraments soon.

The seven sacraments, she explained (pausing), were not a checklist of things I could simply complete, and they were not meant for every person. Choosing her words carefully, she explained I had already completed the sacrament of Baptism as a baby. Now, I will work on the next two, Penance and First Holy Communion. Then comes the sacrament of Confirmation in seventh grade, which she compared to becoming a "soldier for Christ." I would practice being a Christian between my First Holy Communion and the time of my Confirmation.

Confirmation did not sound compelling, as she worded it. Seventh graders must have boring lives, and her reference to soldiers reminded me of dull toys for boys. I told Miss William I did not care about Confirmation, but I still wanted to make all the other sacraments as soon as I could.

She went on to explain Holy Matrimony. My parents had entered into that sacrament, and I could, too, if I wanted to get married when I grew up. Since marriage was for old people, I did not care about that one.

Next, she spoke of Holy Orders for men who become priests. Who cares about that? Holy Orders for old men sounded like the most boring one of them all.

Miss Williams asked me to name the sacraments, and going down the list together, I counted an additional one. Still hopeful, I asked if I could make the last one soon.

"Well, the last one," she said, "is... Extreme Unction." Her voice lowered to a whisper, and she looked me closely in the eye. "Did you ever see, or maybe you might know, like... a really, really, old person lying in their bed in the hospital?"

I nodded.

"Well... Extreme Unction is when a person receives their *last rites*. A priest goes to their bedside and blesses them, and says a prayer for them before they... you know... *die*."

I gulped. "Oh, I... I changed my mind."

THE FOURTEEN STATIONS OF THE CROSS

Miss Williams was a gifted storyteller who knew how to captivate our attention. One day early in the school year, she walked our class over to the church to show us the stained glass Fourteen Stations of the Cross that spanned all along the church wall.

At each stained glass window, she described an event that led to the tragic crucifixion of Jesus. The class was appalled. We all had heard the statement, "Jesus died for us," but usually without emotion.

When we returned to the classroom, Miss Williams was plagued with gory-sounding second-grader questions. Every wound that Jesus suffered, the vinegar-soaked sponge they gave him, and even the Roman soldiers' armor and weaponry stirred up questions from the boys.

My thoughts wandered off to Judas. He was despicable. He betrayed his best friend, sweet Jesus, and turned him over to the Roman soldiers for a puny pouch of 30 pieces of silver—with a *kiss*—to be *brutally murdered!*

After patiently answering everyone's questions, Miss Williams turned our attention to the resurrection. Jesus suffered and took those wounds so he could live in our hearts when we made our First Holy Communion.

THROUGH THE EYES OF JESUS

Throughout the school year after that, Miss Williams frequently inspired our class to look at the world through the eyes of Jesus. She found a way to inject a spiritual lesson into nearly every subject, to prepare us for the big day at the end of the school year.

One such lesson was about abbreviations. She wrote on the blackboard: "i.e. means *id est.* This is a Latin phrase that means, 'that is... for YOU... to say.'"

She explained how people used it in writing and legal documents, and then she added a spiritual lesson. "You can also think of the 'i' as your spirit and the 'e' as your ego. Your spirit says to your ego, 'That is, for YOU to understand (something) like this. The 'i' is first because when you follow Jesus, you always put your spirit before your ego. If you see things with your spirit first, then your ego will understand. And, that way, you will always see others through the eyes of Jesus."

Miss Williams ended the lesson with a little song to aid our memory: "You put your I before your ego, that is, for you, to say!"

Another time, Miss Williams joined the other second-grade teacher to give us an unexpected, all-day lesson on prejudice. The teachers divided the two classes according to eye color when the day began.

All morning, the teacher of the brown-eyed class gave her students many privileges. They did not have to do any schoolwork and had a long recess outside. They talked out loud in class, sang songs, and played games. The teacher even gave them cookies to eat at their desks.

Meanwhile, the teacher of the blue- and green-eyed class made her students do schoolwork quietly from lessons in their books. The classroom doors were open, and both classes could see what the other class was doing across the hall.

Then, after lunchtime, the teachers switched classes. Now the blue- and green-eyed students had all the privileges, while the brown-eyed students had to do schoolwork quietly from lessons in their books.

At the end of the school day and back in our usual classroom, Miss Williams started a discussion about prejudices and discrimination. The class erupted with feelings about how it felt as the discriminated ones, and as the privileged while also knowing the other class was getting unfair treatment. Miss Williams concluded: "When you follow Jesus, you always remember that God is in every person, and you must treat everyone fairly. No matter the color of someone's eyes or skin or whatever they look like on the outside, God is in everyone."

Miss Williams was the perfect role model of what a Christian should be. By the end of the school year, I felt fully prepared to make my First Holy Communion.

Chapter 20

First Holy Communion Day

He took a loaf of bread, and when he had given
thanks, he broke it and gave it to them, saying,
"This is my body, which is given for you. Do
this in remembrance of me."
—Luke 22:19

MAY 29, 1965 WAS A SUNNY AND BREEZY day and the most important day of my life. I barely slept the night before.

Mama took me to her bedroom to fix my hair and help me dress in my formal outfit. She said I looked like a bride going to a wedding. She knew how much I had eagerly anticipated the event.

Then she put her hand under my chin and looked me in the eye. "When you make your First Holy Communion, offer it up with a special intention for me, okay?"

Mama prayed a lot, and sometimes she would say she was praying for a "special intention," a mysterious phrase she could never explain clearly. So, I asked her what it meant. In only slightly different words, she repeated her request that I offer up my First Holy Communion with a special intention for her. So, I said I would.

THE CEREMONY

The ceremony at the church was very large. The second-graders from our school congregated with the second-grade Catholic children in the parish from the public school. A small group of adults also joined us. About 135 parishioners made their First Holy Communion that morning.

I received my Holy Communion at the altar and then returned to my seat and knelt. I shut my eyes and asked Jesus to live inside my heart. I imagined he came through my throat, settled into my heart and grew very big, then filled my whole body.

My heart was pounding inside my chest. It welled up so big that it almost took my breath away. My whole body was tingling with electricity. I hid my face from my classmates around me so they would not see the unstoppable flow of tears, running down my cheeks. Jesus was now living right inside of me, *right inside my heart.*

Then I remembered Mama's special intention, so I asked God for something special for her, too.

THE PHOTOGRAPHY STUDIO

After the ceremony at the church, Mama and Daddy took us to have a family picture taken at a photography studio in the city. We had never had a family picture taken at a studio before. It was a very rare and celebratory treat.

(Back): Helen, Joey, Mike, Mickey, Barbara, Brenda
Donna, Daddy, Mama, Nancy, Tommy, Mary

MAMA'S SPECIAL INTENTION

As soon as we got home, Mama was eager to talk to me alone in her bedroom again. "Well? Tell me about your First Holy Communion! How was it?"

I told her how I asked Jesus to live inside my heart. How he went down my throat and then grew so big in my heart and filled my whole body with electricity.

"And...? Did you remember what I asked, about the special intention for me?"

I nodded.

"Well... ? Won't you tell me? What did you say?" she prodded.

"I asked God to give you a bottle of perfume."

"A bottle of *perfume?!*" Mama scowled a little. She explained her special intention was not a material request for herself. Instead, she wanted to be assured I would always follow Jesus, for her.

I told her I would.

THE BIG PARTY

Then the celebration began. We had a party at our house that was the size of a *wedding!* Our huge family of relatives all came, including oodles of cousins and many friends. They even brought many gifts for me. I felt so rich from the $56 they gave me, tucked in beautiful cards. This was the most money I had ever had in my *entire life!* I thanked them, every one.

Pink and white streamers decorated our yard. A feast lay across a row of tables on the lawn, full of delicious dishes made by Mama and the guests.

Mama took me over to the middle table to present a special cake from Aunt Eileen, from a *real bakery*. I gazed down at the white, oversized, rectangular cake with my name scrolling across it in big pink cursive script. And all around the corners of the cake were frostings of large pink and white roses.

The fabulous party went on all afternoon. There were no limits on how much food, desserts, or soda pop we could have. Old people were playing horseshoes on the lawn. Grownups were yakking and laughing as they mingled about in groups. Teenagers were in the basement playing the Limbo Rock song on our tall, antique, black marble jukebox, and the boys were holding the broomstick for the girls, lining up in a row to take turns dancing under it. Little kids were swinging on the swing set, playing games, and chasing each other all around the property. People were everywhere, having fun.

Then, as the evening approached and the party dwindled, I passed by two of my uncles sitting on a picnic bench in the yard. I overheard one say to the other, "Look at Jimmy over there. He's had one too many beers. He's really drunk."

I learned about drinking during that school year while watching three movies. Daddy was strict about what we younger kids could watch on television. We had to turn the channel if he believed something was inappropriate for our age. But when Mama and Daddy were not at home, my oldest sister, Mickey, insisted we watch adult movies she liked, such as *The Days of Wine and Roses*, *Cat on a Hot Tin Roof*, and *Your Cheatin' Heart* (the rise and fall of country singer Hank Williams).

All three were scary movies about how drinking caused people's lives to fall apart and marriages to break up. I learned from them about drunkenness for the first time. Based on these movies, I thought only wine or whiskey made people drunk. Daddy did not drink wine or whiskey, however, he only drank beer.

So, upon hearing my uncle's remark, I went over by Daddy to find out if he was drunk. He was sitting on a picnic bench in another area of the yard, all alone. As I attempted to pass by him, he stopped me by holding out an empty beer bottle to my chest. Slurring his words, he asked, "Donna, would you get me another beer?"

I froze.

He was half falling off the bench, holding the bottle to my chest, and reeking heavily of beer. His face looked contorted, and his eyes were rolling and half shut.

I was so upset that I could not bear to look at Daddy. I always did what he asked, but I turned and ran away this time. And as I ran, he laughed and snidely slurred at my reaction. "Ha! Ha! Oh, so now she doesn't want to *get it for me?*"

I tried to find a place to be alone, to cry for a little while, but there was no quiet place anywhere. So, I ran to find my next two older sisters, Barbara and Brenda, and called them to a club meeting in our bedroom closet. I told them about seeing Daddy drunk. Could beer make a person drunk as wine or whiskey did?

They laughed. "Yeah, beer makes people drunk! *Sure* it does!" Barbara said. "He gets drunk all the *time* with beer. That's how he gets his kicks. *Didn't you know that?*

Just watch him, watch him... *you'll* see—he does it all the *time*, I tell ya... he does it all the time."

FIRST HOLY COMMUNION WOUNDS

To see Daddy stone drunk and to learn of his drinking habit was a deep and sudden shock. The happiest day of my life, the one I had been waiting and preparing for an entire school year, became the saddest, the very moment Daddy held out that beer bottle to my chest. I had reached the top of a mountain that day and then tumbled straight down off a cliff. My spiritual joy had vanished, and painful wounds appeared.

I cried in bed that night until the next morning. My eyes were sore and puffy, and I could not breathe. I soaked my pillow with tears and curled up in a ball because my ribs and stomach muscles were sore from sobbing. My heart was aching as I had never felt before. I clutched my chest and worried I might have a heart attack. I wondered if Jesus felt like this when they stabbed him in the heart.

Then the next day, Mama went to the store and left Mickey in charge. Mickey was usually at the center of family discord and always seeking attention. She was very jealous of Mama's favorable opinion of me, and that family relatives said I resembled Mama in her looks and ways.

Whenever Mickey caused trouble, she would cry to Mama that "things" bothered her and caused "problems with [her] nerves" to gain her sympathy and escape responsibility. Mama was too softhearted to see Mickey's deep contempt for me, and that her emotional problems were jealousy and hatred of her own making.

When Mama was at the store, Mickey would not let me get a drink of water in the kitchen. She started a physical fight with me and grabbed a paring knife from the silverware drawer. When I saw the knife, I ran to get away from her, but she chased me up the bedroom stairs. She stabbed me in the palm of my right hand, from behind me on the stairs. My hand started bleeding heavily, and a black vein protruded from my palm.

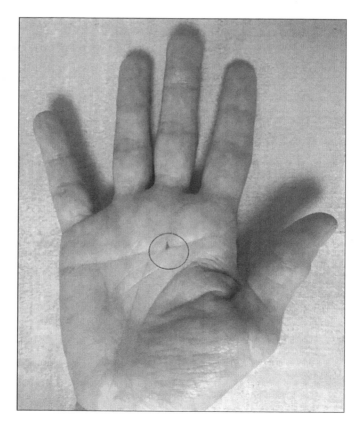

When Mama came home, I tried to tell her what had happened, but Mickey spoke over me and lied. She said I purposely pushed her while she was peeling potatoes and claimed it was an accident on her part.

It was no accident. Mickey was 13, and I was seven. She started a physical fight and grabbed a knife for a weapon. She had no reason to chase me with a knife, up the stairs, other than to hurt me.

Mama bandaged my hand, and I needed a full bandage for several weeks. I carried a permanent visible scar from the attack, just under the skin.

I cried in bed that night, and Mama came up to comfort me. She started by trying to say Mickey really loves me but "has problems with—"

Mickey did not love me. She hated me. I quickly interrupted Mama and held out my bandaged hand. "Did she stab *me*, or did she stab Jesus?"

Mama stared blankly at me. She could not answer my question in a way that would also defend Mickey. After a moment of silence, she attempted to deny Mickey's responsibility. "Well, she didn't mean—"

I interrupted her again and held out my bandaged hand. I reminded her that Jesus was inside me from the day before. "If Jesus is inside me, then she stabbed Jesus there, too. If Jesus is inside a person and someone hurts them, they must also hurt Jesus in the same place, right?"

Mama repeatedly tried to defend Mickey, and every time, I held out my bandaged hand and only repeated the same questions, to which she did not answer. I could only see it literally: Mickey must have hurt Jesus if she hurt me.

Finally, Mama said, "Donna, there's something very special about you. You understand things about God that other people don't. You are a peacemaker. So, I'm asking if you will always be the peacemaker in our family, for me. And pray that, one day, Mickey will understand things about Jesus as you do."

I told her I would.

CHAPTER 21

THE GRAVEYARD TOUR

What is your life? For you are a mist that appears
for a little while and then vanishes.
—Jas 4:14b

A FEW WEEKS LATER, on the first Sunday of summer vacation, our family went to a lawn fête at Saint Mary's Church, out in the country. My big brothers' teenage band was playing their first gig there.

Toward the evening, I wandered off alone, down a hill, and into the edge of the church cemetery. Right away, a maze of narrow paths drew me in, so I could read tombstones for the first time in my life. I only knew of one person who had died in my lifetime before then. The year before, the hushed death of my Grandpa Leo had occurred.

A lone walk through a graveyard at dusk seemed quite spooky, yet equally intriguing. I was entering a territory of lingering ghosts, I thought, but a kind of "holy land" as well.

My first solo graveyard tour required a lot of courage. So, I decided if I took God with me and talked to him along the way, he would keep me safe. I made a deal with God. I would pray for some of the dead and their families if he would protect me from any ghosts. With that, I dared to venture further inside.

As I began trailing through rows and rows of similar flat gray slabs, and weary-looking, upright-standing stones, I imagined who some of the departed strangers might have been, with their quaint names. What might they once have looked like, and what had their stories been? I calculated the number of years some people had walked on earth. Some had lived for about 95 years or more and died 100 years before my time.

"Those are some real antiques you have up there," I said to God. Then, I thought, "But no matter how long they ever, *ever* lived... they're just bones in boxes now, below the flat, gray stones at my feet."

They reminded me of Ash Wednesday, the first day of Lent, at the church. Father Doyle took some sweet-smelling ashes and smudged a cross on my forehead with his thumb. "From ashes to ashes, and from dust to dust, you shall return!" he proclaimed.

I came to the grave of a girl the same age as me who had died on her birthday. I felt sad for her. I was expecting presents on my upcoming birthday, and she got *death* on hers. It was a scary thought that death could also happen to me. Death could happen to *anyone*, at any time. I said a quick prayer for the girl as I hurried along.

At the grave of a baby, I wondered how the child, so young, had died. I imagined the precious little infant in the arms of his wailing mother. She had to let him go, on that sad day, the date engraved on the baby's stone.

Next, I came upon seven people, all from one family, buried side by side. I pictured them long ago, laughing and talking and playing cards, sitting together around a kitchen table. And now they were all silent and still, lying together around the shady trees of the cemetery.

Sooner or later, it *all* ends. No matter *who* had been the king of their hill or *who* had won the card game, everyone winds up in the same quiet graveyards, like the one where I was standing.

Occasionally, I passed by graves of shiny marble towering above the others. They looked like monuments or business buildings in miniature. "It's the grave of a rich, old businessman," I thought, each time I passed by one of these monuments.

I wondered if the dead, rich, old businessmen under their shiny monuments were luckier for where they had gone in the spirit world, forever—luckier, that is, than the poor, forgotten souls resting under the tiny slabs nearby, half covered by grass.

In the whole cemetery, just a few of the graves had statues of angels over them, big and pretty. These grave owners were the luckiest of the dead, the most blessed of all. I wondered if they got to go to the highest of heavenly places. After all, they were the dead, the rich, *and* the holy ones. What could be better than that?

The most interesting part of my graveyard tour was discovering a few virtuous words on some of the cemetery stones. A word or two whispered something timeless about the person whose name was on the stone, with their two fixed dates underneath.

EULA, LOVING, said one. A picture of Eula, a sweet, pudgy grandma, flashed in my head. I imagined she was pulling a fresh apple pie from her oven. Grandma Eula always had a dessert ready for when family and friends came to visit.

HERMAN, THE FAITHFUL, said another. Under the nearby tree, I sensed the spirit of a skinny, smiling old man in a rocking chair, reading his Holy Bible. Herman was a friendly spirit, but he spooked me a little. I said a quick prayer for him as I moved on.

While reading the strangers' tombstones, I began to wonder what calendar date in history I would die myself. What words would be on my tombstone, inscribed for eternity about me?

I stopped to ask, "God, why do you let people die, anyhow?" Right away, I answered my question so God would not think I was accusing him of being mean. "I know. You let people die to make more room on earth for the new people." I spoke as to let God off the hook.

I imagined myself like the little black ant I had played with in the grass that morning. There I was, crawling around on earth like billions of others on a brief June day in 1965. My life was just a single point and a teeny-weeny dot in time. I was no more than a microscopic speck the world could surely do without.

I wondered why I even existed, and what my life's purpose could possibly be. How could I ever make any difference to the world at all? "Am I to grow up and have babies?" I thought. But then, why wouldn't God skip over me and just let Mama have my babies? I did not know.

It was almost dark. I looked all around the graveyard, and in a loud voice, I asked, *"Why was I born, God? Why am I here?"*

CHAPTER 22

SIXTEEN ROSARIES

Trust in the LORD with all your heart, and do not
rely on your own insight.
—Proverbs 3:5

MY WHOLE WORLD changed after I made my First
Holy Communion. Daddy was a different person.
Before that day, everything was okay when he was just
being strict. But now he was acting just like the drunk men
in the movies.

Before my First Communion, I had never heard
Mama and Daddy fighting. Then, after I became aware of
the problem, I often heard them fighting late at night after
I went to bed. I tried to listen to their fights to foreknow the
fate that would befall our family. Sometimes, Daddy said he
might leave us.

Despite my fears about Daddy, I always said hello
when he stumbled through the door after work. That he still
came home, and returned my greeting, seemed like
reassuring signs that he still cared about our family.

Mickey began provoking Daddy into anger with her bad behavior frequently then, too. They were constantly battling. Sometimes after they fought, Mickey would chide me. "Well? Do you hate him yet?"

"No, I don't hate him."

"Well, you just wait—*you will!*"

I continually worried my parents might get a divorce and our family would fall apart. Where would Daddy go? I feared he would disappear and I would never see him again. Who would give us haircuts? How would we get food? Divorce was very uncommon in 1965, and I worried about what people would think of our family. I cried in bed for hours over these anxieties throughout the summer. And I prayed for Daddy every night.

I made a deal with God. I told him if he would get Daddy to stop drinking, and stop the fighting in the house, then I would pray a rosary every night for God, from then on—for life.

As Daddy's drinking and the fights continued, I quickly became impatient, waiting for God to answer. So, I increased my offer to two rosaries for God. Then three, four... five... nine... twelve...

But God was very quiet the whole summer and did not answer. I resolved to still pray the rosaries I promised to him, to keep my end of the bargain, even if God had not come through, yet.

Sometimes, Mama heard me crying in bed and came upstairs to comfort me. Then, one night at summer's end, she came again after a chaotic day in the house.

I told her all about the rosaries I had promised God if he would stop Daddy from drinking and stop the fighting in the house. By then, I was up to 16 rosaries a night and kept falling asleep before I even finished the first ten beads of the first one. So, I was feeling very guilty, too, for not keeping my promise to God.

Then Mama said, "Donna, there's something very special about you. You are a peacemaker. Keep praying for Daddy. You might not see it now, but one day you will know that God has heard your prayers."

I told her I would.

CHAPTER 23

BACK TO THE PRAYER OF SAINT FRANCIS

I love the LORD, because he has heard my voice and
my supplications. Because he inclined his ear to
me, therefore I will call on him as long as I live.
—Ps 116:1-2

SO DURING A PRAYER in 2005, three years after he
had died, Daddy showed me everything, appearing
from heaven.

I remembered how Miss Williams had prepared me
throughout the school year for that long-awaited day of
May 29, 1965. And the indescribable joy when I received
my First Holy Communion that morning. An event so
significant that we even went to a photography studio in the
city for pictures.

And I remembered all the details of the grand party
that was the size of a wedding. The banquet and streamers,
the laughter, the dancing, and games. I felt rich for the first

time in my life that day. And like I was somebody special, when I looked down at the enormous bakery cake with the large pink and white roses, surrounding my name.

Then how I cried the whole night after the party and into the next morning, and worried about having a heart attack. And the summer of tears that followed, full of unfinished rosaries, as I begged to a silent God.

After remembering all of it, I sat immersed in thought for a while. I had been in a trance.

Then Daddy's spirit came to me in the room. I saw him in a small picture, like the framed miniature visible through a telescope. Daddy looked like a wavy figure, and his vibration pulsing through the atmosphere became stronger and stronger.

He said to me, "Please forgive me for the time when you were seven, and your image of me fell... when you could no longer bear to look at me, so you turned and ran away... when I broke the Sacred Heart of Jesus on your First Holy Communion Day."

CHAPTER 24

MEMORIES

I thank my God every time I remember you.
—Phil 1:3

A PECULIAR THING HAPPENED after that. Over the following months, many distant memories of Daddy appeared. Random downloads played, out of the blue, like reels of film on an old movie projector.

Memories of Daddy went back to my very early childhood. Scenes with remarkable details displayed his pleasant emotions and magnified the loving side of his character.

Throughout my childhood, after I got ready for bed, Daddy would sit in the kitchen, waiting for a kiss and hug good night. He would always say, "Say your prayers, God bless you, good night."

I noticed his generosity when I realized Daddy seldom spent money on himself. He had a small collection of Johnny Cash albums, but never bought himself a record player to listen to them. He had no male hobbies or toys like other men, and he and Mama rarely had new clothes. They both sacrificed a lot for our family.

On Christmas morning, when I was in seventh grade, our entire living room was full of gifts Daddy had made. There was a train set and a rocking horse for my little brothers and a bright red desk for me.

A humorous third-grade incident reminded me of how Daddy cared about my schoolwork. He was the one who insisted on signing my school papers, so I dreaded the day I came home with a poor grade on a test. *How could I get out of this?*

So, I got the foolish idea to trick my oldest brother, Joey, into signing my test paper, since he was named after Daddy. I put my hand over my poor grade and asked him to show me his signature at the top of the paper. But Joey tricked me instead and, pressing hard, scribbled on my paper. Then he roared, laughing when I tore a hole in my paper, trying to erase it. So, I had to get Daddy's signature, after all. He lectured me about doing well in school and grounded me from watching television for a week, so I could use that time studying instead.

As a child, I had always thought Daddy's concern for my schoolwork was just another one of his harsh ways. But he motivated me to do well in school since I did not want to face the consequences of getting poor grades.

Daddy was a proud father. He always carried a family picture in his wallet and pulled it out occasionally to show others.

In my early childhood, our family car was a big, old, red and white, retired ambulance car with unusual backward side doors. Daddy loved it whenever we stopped at a red light in our ambulance car, and the people behind us would try to count our heads. Sometimes, the driver would shout out to ask Daddy, "All yours?"

"Yep! They're all mine!" Daddy would shout back with a laugh.

Daddy was proud of my big brothers when they formed their teenage band, the Modernaires. He was excited to inform them he would be their agent, and it was he who arranged their first official gig at the Saint Mary's lawn fête out in the country.

Unlike other families, our large family could not go on vacations or to the movies or restaurants. I did not go out for entertainment much as a child other than occasionally visiting relatives. But Mama and Daddy always took us on family outings whenever possible. My childhood experiences may seem commonplace to many today, but they were special to a child growing up in a big family in the 1960s.

Daddy had an ice cream addiction. Sometimes, on hot summer evenings, we all piled into the car and headed out to Jim's Ice Cream Stand by the lake for giant ice cream cones. I could barely hold them; they were that big.

Chestnut Ridge Park, full of tall shady trees, was my favorite place for our family picnics. I loved rolling down the cliffs in the crisp leaves and playing on the park rides.

And every summer, Mama and Daddy frequently took us to the beach. We had so many good times there. Daddy loved the water. He gave swimming lessons to whoever he could coax and always helped Mama to float.

We had our share of annual family outings as well. We always took a trip to the zoo and attended the Barnum & Bailey Circus some winters when it came to town. The clowns on stilts, the dancing elephants, and the acrobats doing backward somersaults on the high wire and going hand-to-hand on their flying trapeze high above the ground kept me on the edge of my seat.

My favorite annual outing was at the Crystal Beach Amusement Park in Canada. Going on all the rides was thrilling, and eating hot dogs and long, crispy French fries sprinkled with vinegar at the stands was a treat. The carnival noises, colorful flashing lights everywhere, and the sights of many unusual characters had me spellbound.

While the family ran into the Spook House, I always lagged behind until Joey came back out to get me. I had to stop and study the Laughing Lady, which stood behind the large glass window at the entrance.

The Laughing Lady was a giant lady with red curly hair, clad in a black and white polka-dot dress. She was a little scary, but it was safe to watch her because she was behind the glass. Her body shook and shook as she kept laughing and looking down at me. I was too young to distinguish fantasy from reality, so I could only sense some strange vibe emanating from her robotic body. Was she human? Bewildered, I did not know. Or if not human, then what *was* she?

Niagara Falls, Canada

(Left): Mama holding Mary, Donna, Helen, Brenda
(Right): Mike, Nancy, Joey, Mickey, Barbara

And we always visited Niagara Falls in Canada annually. After viewing the rainbows in the spectacular waterfalls, we explored the museums. Mama and Daddy loved telling us about how they spent their honeymoon in Niagara Falls.

A VISIT TO THE RISINGVILLE FARM

When I was four, Daddy took our family on a visit to a farm where he had a remodeling job for the farmer. I was only familiar with farms from storybooks, cartoons, and television before then, so I expected to see some combination of the scenes and characters I already knew. Such a visit would satisfy my intense curiosity about what a farm would be like.

As its name implied, at the Risingville Farm, the sun will be rising, and the farmer will be milking his cows. It will be a very pretty farm, with meandering wooden fences, and a friendly dog, like Lassie, will run up and greet us. Mother hens will be strutting around the chicken yard with their baby chicks following behind, and a big, white, bossy rooster like Foghorn Leghorn will be minding the fort. There will be cute little, rosy-pink pigs with curly tails, like Porky and his friends. I will get to ride on a horse, or even ride on Mr. Ed, the talking horse on my favorite television show, if he's there.

When we arrived at the farm, the farmer, his wife, and their 11-year-old boy stood in the driveway, smiling and waving at us. But we had to stay in the car until the farmer boy locked up their two large, ferocious, barking black dogs in their dog shed so they wouldn't bite us.

First, the farmer boy took us inside a big fence to see the cows. The rusty wire fence, lined with sharp little nails, grabbed me by my pretty, ruffled blouse and ripped a hole in it.

The cows stood still in the fields in the hot sun, swatting swarms of flies off their big bodies with their tails. We didn't get too close to them because we didn't want to step in their stinky doo-doo.

Next, the farmer boy showed us a gigantic pigsty, packed with huge, smelly pigs. The big fat pigs grunted loudly and wallowed in deep, soupy mud. Patchy pink and brown spots dotted their skin all over and looked like a painful rash. They splashed mud all around, and some got all over my pretty blouse.

Then I asked the farmer boy to take me to ride the horses. "No horses here," he snapped. "This ain't a *horse* farm. This is a *pig* farm."

So, I wandered off alone and discovered a fenced-in chicken yard behind the barn. Just like in cartoons, mama hens were parading around the inside edge of the yard, and oodles of little chicks were following them.

When I caught sight of all the furry, yellow baby chicks, I thought I could catch one to take home with me and let it live under my bed. Now, I had the perfect chance to have a baby animal to love, small enough for me to hold. So, I opened the gate and began running around the chicken yard to catch a little chick.

Then a small black rooster started moving around, scratching the ground, and crowing like crazy. And the mama hens began running and jumping in the air, clucking loudly and flapping their wings. The baby chicks all started running and squeaking behind them.

Then everyone came and circled outside the chicken yard, and they were shouting. Joey came in and picked me up, carried me over his shoulder, and set me down by Mama. Mickey rushed over and kept poking me in my side with her finger, saying over and over, "You're *mean!* How would *you* like it if somebody tried to take *you* away from *your* mother, *huh? Shame* on you! You're *mean!*"

All I knew was I was trying to catch a little animal to love, one I could hold. I wouldn't hurt it, but only love it and keep it under my bed. Since I could not explain my intentions to anyone, I just cried and kept saying inside my head, "I just wanted to catch a little chick!"

While lying in bed that night, I reflected on the stark differences between reality and my great expectations of the day. The farm dogs were dangerous—the kind that *attack* people. The fence with the nails grabbed me and ripped my pretty blouse. I had to plug my nose near the stinky cows, and the big smelly pigs with a rash splashed mud all over me. I didn't get to ride a horse, and Mr. Ed wasn't there. And I didn't catch a little chick to live under my bed.

Yet, I was quite content since my curiosity had been satisfied. I had reached a milestone, and I was growing up. For the first time in my life, I was on a farm.

DEAR HEART

When I was three, Daddy taught me about last names one day. "The Busshart family, my grandparents, came from Germany. In Germany, 'BUSS' means deer like the animal, and a 'HART' is a father deer.

"And 'DEAR' is a word we say for a special person, and a 'HEART' is like an 'I love you' heart." Then he cupped his hands before me and said, "So, Donna Marie Busshart, I give you my dear heart."

NEW SHOES AND ANKLES

When I was two, Daddy burst through the back door of the kitchen one day, all excited, and announced he was taking us all out to get new shoes. A lady in a shoe store had said he could buy shoes for all his kids for fifty cents a pair. So, we all packed into the ambulance car to travel to a small and crowded shoe store in the city.

While Mama helped my siblings choose their shoes, Daddy set me on a chair at the front of the store to put a stark white pair of new toddler shoes on me. As he laced them up, he said we could not choose another kind, like my siblings, because I needed the same style as my old pair for my ankles. As he put them on me, he kept rubbing the sides of my feet and saying over and over that the new shoes would strengthen my ankles.

At two, whenever I discovered anything new, I believed it had just been made, as if it did not exist before my discovery. I had never noticed my ankles on my body before Daddy did that, so I believed I was getting new ankles along with my new shoes. For the rest of the day, I kept admiring my snowy-white new shoes, and bending down to feel my new ankles under them.

PORRIDGE

It was nighttime, and Daddy and I were home alone. I stood by him at the stove, holding onto his pant leg, while he made us warm milk with butter and sugar over bread. Daddy was singing. "Mama has a new baby, and her name is Nancy..."

The dish was porridge, he said, like the kind eaten in my favorite storybook, "Goldilocks and the Three Bears."

Then, he put me in my high chair, and we ate at the kitchen table together. Making the spoon like an airplane, he put it in my mouth. The porridge was delicious.

Such loving memories of Daddy, now magnified, went all the way back to the first time I ever saw his face.

BAPTISM 1957

I felt like I was merely a torso, or a small, white beam of light, floating in the dark. A long white gown with short ruffled sleeves pinched the tops of my arms and faded into the space below.

Through gray, fuzzy film, I watched black shadows in an outer layer encircle me. They made soft sounds together, like uniform chants.

All things in the realm of the shadows were cold and dark and either black or dim-white. I did not care or wonder what any of it meant. The darkness, their chants, the long white gown, and the smell of cold water all signified a ritual I should quietly endure.

Then, I felt warmth from behind me, and I turned from the dark corner where the shadows dwelt. In the distance behind were brilliant rays of colors shining down, bursting through a prism from somewhere high above. From one light, myriad lively, warm hues were spattering down, giving life to a large, dim, stony brown place.

I only caught a glimpse of the dazzling lights when the firm hands that held me fought to turn my torso back around. Again and again, I squirmed to defy them. All I knew was that I wanted to see the warm and beautiful colored lights.

Yet, the hands forced me to surrender and face the cold, dark corner instead. Then they moved me forward, and I looked down to the center of a round, white basin with a curly edge. I shivered in the coolness of the dark as large cold droplets of water fell from my crown and into the vessel below.

Then, the chanting and the dark ceremony abruptly stopped, and a figure came toward me to take me from the hands. I recognized the warm, flesh-colored hands that reached for me, by the shiny gold wedding ring with the big, blue aquamarine stone. As the ring came closer, the figure transformed into the handsome, dark-haired man I knew as Daddy.

Noise and movement filled the air then, and Daddy blended into the colored picture of an altogether different room in the daylight. He wrestled with the long, white gown that had twisted around me and put a white blanket over me. Farther away, my siblings circled around Mama in the aisle as they put on their coats.

Daddy raised me to the shoulder of his light brown suit, and I studied the side of his face. As we headed toward the door, I looked up to a warm light touching my forehead. And as we passed through the light, I saw the beautiful kaleidoscope of colors, coming from a high, stained glass window of the church.

CONCLUSION

We know we have reached the stage of truly forgiving someone when we can see what they did *for* us, rather than *to* us. Since those tender childhood memories of Daddy, he randomly sends occasional reminders I know could only be from him.

A most phenomenal time was in a hotel room while visiting with friends. My portable CD player, loaded with a CD of 100 random songs, sat on a cabinet across the room, and the player was off. As I began telling my friends about some crazy thing Daddy once did, the CD player turned on, all by itself, playing his favorite song, "Imagine."

Although he is in heaven now, I feel a stronger bond with Daddy than ever before. I am grateful for everything that transpired in my relationship with him, which ultimately has led me to a higher spiritual plateau.

Chapter 25

The Eyes of Jesus

For "In him we live and move and have our being";
as even some of your own poets have said,
"For we too are his offspring."
—Acts 17:28

ONE YEAR AFTER I prayed the prayer of St. Francis and experienced the vision and memories of Daddy, I was living back in Knoxville, Tennessee. My new apartment was in a peaceful setting on the outskirts of the city. From the balcony, pine trees were in view, covering the park grounds below. Beyond the pines extended a branch of the beautiful Tennessee River. Sometimes, at the break of dawn, I sat on the balcony to watch a man playing his flute on the river in his canoe.

One afternoon, I fell asleep on the couch, in my living room, near the balcony. As the afternoon passed, the sun came over the building, and bright rays of light shone down on me into the room. I tossed in my sleep, trying to keep the sunlight out of my face.

When I could no longer avoid the light, I opened my eyes to look out at the sky. And in the clouds, smiling down from heaven was Daddy's face, radiant and large, with a bright halo around his head.

Then he suddenly appeared above me at the couch, towering over me like a giant, yet also somewhat at a distance. Daddy was dressed like a Catholic nun, in a black gown, a long black veil, and a white linen square on his forehead. He had a very large wooden rosary around his waist.

He was smiling so big, bigger than a human smile, as he looked down into my eyes. His eyes were glowing with an indescribable look, saturated with love. Then, he took the large cross on his rosary and, reaching down, touched my forehead with it.

His eyes remained steadfast, looking into mine, while his face started changing, and then kept going back and forth... back and forth... First, the face was Daddy... then it was Jesus... then it was Daddy... then it was Jesus...

I silently stared, looking up into his intensely loving eyes as tears rolled down and soaked my pillow. I just kept whispering inside with awe, "Is it Daddy?... or is it Jesus?... is it Daddy?... or is it Jesus?" I really could not tell.

CHAPTER 26

ABOUT THE THORNS

We know that all things work together for good
for those who love God, who are called
according to his purpose.
—Rom 8:28

WHEN MISS WILLIAMS told the story of Jesus'
crucifixion in second grade, I harshly judged Judas
for his part. I remember wishing to punish him for what he
had done to Jesus. Selling out his best friend with a false
kiss for a piddly bit of money to be brutally murdered was
unthinkable. He could be nothing more than a greedy, evil,
heartless traitor.

But suppose Judas had not betrayed Jesus, and
suppose Pontius Pilate had set him free. What if Jesus had
spent his life walking around in a white robe and sandals
and preaching in parks about God instead? And then he
just died of natural causes at the ripe old age of 120?

The whole purpose of the crucifixion of Jesus was to
forgive us and for the spiritual enlightenment, redemption,

and ascension of all humanity. Somebody had to be the Judas in that story for Jesus to fulfill his mission. In that light, I can see Judas' betrayal was actually a great sacrifice for us all rather than a terrible deed.

The Purpose of a Pain

When you love somebody, you want others to see the person's good side as you do. So, you want to protect your loved one from judgment if others hear something negative about them. And you do not want to be the one to expose your loved one's downfalls or shortcomings.

I really struggled at times while writing the story about Daddy. I did not want to tell you about his abusive behavior and drunkenness because I did not want you to judge him. Instead, I wanted you, the reader, to love him. So, I tried to write the story without mentioning his terrible deeds, or at least by only slightly alluding to them. Yet, each time, I had to get away from writing until I could figure out how to get around the sad truth.

Then, I would see Daddy as he used to be, holding out his arms and shouting, "Just tell it like it is, right?"

If I had told it otherwise, the story would not be his story, the story about Daddy. And the message in his story would be much more important to Daddy than anyone's judgment of him.

More About The Sheep and the Goats

Now, as I reach this point in the book, the parable of the sheep and the goats deserves further reckoning. We are not only to show kindness to strangers on buses and at red lights and in prisons, but also to those closest to us, the ones we often take for granted or overlook.

Oh, what do I really know? I have been so blind. As this book progressed, I gradually realized Daddy was the one who had been teaching *me* about Jesus all along.

Jesus was the needy one who I turned away when we had our last misunderstanding. And the sick one, who I did not visit in the nursing home down the road from me before he died.

All throughout my life, Jesus came to me, and I failed to recognize him. I really, never knew it was him.

Jesus came to me through my father, a carpenter named Joseph. He was the one who reached for me at my Baptism and carried me through a church. He fed me some porridge when I was one, and bought me some shoes that came with new ankles at two. He held out his hands to give me his dear heart when I was three.

Jesus was the one who sang a little song on my porch that time in Tennessee. The same one who stood up crookedly, with tears in his eyes and outstretched arms, and advised we pray for peace on earth.

Once, when I visited Daddy in Waco, Texas, it was Jesus who asked me to teach *him* all about Jesus. And when he motioned to the little plaque on his television, he chuckled. "You gotta keep *looking*, Donna, until you see *Jesus!*"

And Jesus came to me as the beggar that night who felt unworthy of his intensely passionate wish to, one day, tell the whole world about Jesus.

Then Daddy came to me in a vision. He was dressed like a Catholic nun, as if to tell me he had sent me to the Our Lady of the Sacred Heart School so I would learn about the Sacred Heart of Jesus. He touched my forehead with the large cross on his rosary to remind me of Mama's words when I told her about the 16 rosaries: "Keep praying for Daddy. You might not see it now, but one day you will know that God has heard your prayers." And in the same vision, Jesus was Daddy.

REFLECTIONS ON THE ROSE GARDEN VISION

The Rose Garden vision initially puzzled me because Jesus said, "Yes... and you got to wear the flowers that time, and I got to wear the thorns." I wondered why he did not simply say, "You wore the flowers, and I wore the thorns."

Instead, he said it as if we were in a play together and playing our parts interchangeably. Or as if, on another occasion, I might be the one to wear the thorns.

I truly understand the vision now. We all show each other the way in the stories of our lives, by our greater or lesser lights that God has made us to be. In every story, we can shine to become like Judas, or shine our greater light, embodying Jesus Christ. And I got to wear the flowers this time, and Daddy wore the thorns.

CHAPTER 27

FORGIVENESS

Be kind to one another, tenderhearted, forgiving
one another, as God in Christ has forgiven you.
—Eph 4:32

FORGIVENESS MAY BE a process of uncovering many layers, especially when deep-seated wounds are involved. The greater the injury, the more challenging it can be. We must genuinely desire to forgive someone, and we may ask God to show us how to get there. Once I had asked God if the hurt from my unresolved relationship with Daddy meant I had not completely forgiven him, the healing process began.

Resistance causes our pain, and acceptance releases it. Reminding ourselves that we are all human and no one is perfect enables us to accept what has happened, have mercy on the offender, and release our pain. Sometimes, the misdeeds of others may even have a way of paving our path in life to take a turn for the better. Or that individual may have unintentionally played an integral part in our spiritual development.

Some people do not understand what forgiveness is. To forgive is to let go of anger or resentment and relinquish any claim to a debt for the pain or loss we have suffered. Forgiveness is not only something we do for others, but also what we do for ourselves. We cut ties with our anger toward the offender and heal our hearts by releasing deeply held negative feelings.

Forgiveness is not forgetting the past; reconciling; dropping our boundaries with an untrustworthy person; condoning, excusing, or denying the offense; something to hold over someone; and it does not release the offender from their responsibilities or any legal retribution. It is simply releasing resentment for an injustice done to us.

Some believe forgiveness is only possible if the person involved is present, but this is false. We can forgive someone we may never talk to or encounter again, or someone who might not even know they hurt us. And we can forgive others through prayer if we cannot reach them in person or if it is inappropriate. My experience with Daddy illustrates forgiveness is achievable even after a loved one has passed.

When we are the offender, a genuine "I'm sorry" can go a long way if given a chance. Breaking the ice may bring great relief to both parties. We can then heal emotions, better understand one another, and possibly mend the relationship.

If the person is still upset with us, we cannot allow their unwillingness to forgive to hold us back if we are sincere in our feelings and actions. The one who asks for forgiveness is much stronger spiritually than the bitter or proud one who refuses to let go. Through prayer, we can also ask others to forgive us.

Some people, mainly those heavily laden with guilt, find forgiving themselves harder than forgiving others. But if we cannot forgive ourselves, how can we expect God to?

Guilt only leads to self-destructive behaviors, such as depression, addictions, suicide, or harm to others. What we did in our past or what others may think of us does not define us; what defines us is that we learn from our mistakes and what we do from now on. We change our ways for our own sake rather than for the approval of others. As the scripture verifies: "Our purpose is to please God, not people. He alone examines the motives of our hearts" (1 Thess 2:4 NLT). We cannot change the past, no matter what it was, but God is ready to help us start anew.

Sometimes people say they do not know how to forgive someone because the transgression was too terrible. But nothing is impossible with God. A devout Christian acquaintance once expressed her deep concern about her inability to forgive some people who had severely injured her emotionally. She burst into tears because she had tried numerous methods without success and needed to do so before she passed away because of her advanced age. She felt she could not ask God for help and had to work things out on her own, since Christians are supposed to be forgiving people.

Christians do not acquire an instant, magical ability to master forgiveness. It may be challenging for anyone. Many people go through life attempting various forgiveness strategies, never realizing we may seek God's help. We will only please God with our request, since our goal is to become more like Jesus.

THE UNFORGIVING SERVANT

Some people have difficulty forgiving another because they do not believe the other person deserves it. Yet, Jesus died for us all, and none of us deserve it.

In the Gospel of Matthew 18:23–35, Jesus tells the parable of the unforgiving servant. In summary, a merciful king forgives a servant for an enormous debt. Later, the same servant meets up with a fellow servant and refuses to forgive him for a much smaller debt. He ruthlessly grabs his fellow servant by the throat and throws him into prison. When the king learns what the unmerciful servant did, he turns him over to the prison to be tortured.

Jesus sacrificed his life to forgive us for all offenses we have ever done to others. The parable of the unforgiving servant tells us that is only half of the equation. We are not to put our faith in Jesus, only to seize forgiveness for ourselves and then walk away like an unforgiving servant. We are to forgive others for their offenses against us, just as God has forgiven us for ours. This is not optional, but a spiritual principle we must live by.

Even so, the most challenging people to forgive are those who show no remorse or deny their offenses. Many people in this world will never, ever admit their mistakes or ever say they are sorry. Some even laugh at their own heartlessness. So, we will only sometimes get the apology we deserve. We can find peace and freedom by forgiving others, or hold our resentment to punish them as prisoners.

But as the parable teaches, we will also end up imprisoned by holding others as our prisoners.

CONCLUSION

Forgiveness is a spiritual act that takes place in the heart and, therefore, is a crucial part of our spiritual journey. Our decision to forgive or refuse will either distance us from God or bring us closer to him.

The transgressions of others can turn our hearts to stone, and forgiveness is the only cure. We must remove the stones that the offenses leave behind. And by removing the stones, we protect our hearts and cultivate our spiritual gardens in heaven.

Not only did Jesus come to forgive us, but also to teach us how to forgive others. When we live in our ego nature, we center on ourselves, making forgiveness difficult. When we live in our spiritual nature by following Jesus, we develop Christlike compassion for others, which increases our ability to forgive. We advance spiritually, moving on to a happier, more productive, and peaceful life and bringing peace to others on earth.

CHAPTER 28

THE BEGGAR'S WISH

What is impossible for mortals is possible for God.
—Luke 18:27

Then his jaw dropped, and his eyes got big and
glassy... "Oh! Can you imagine if together we
could come up with a way to tell the whole
world about Jesus? Wouldn't that be fun? Oh,
how I would love to do that with you
someday!"
—Daddy, Waco, Texas, 1986

EVERYBODY IS SOMEBODY to Jesus. I could never
have imagined there would ever be a way to grant
Daddy his beggar's wish, and I have always admired him
for what it was. He reminded me of when the Lord asked
King Solomon in a dream what he would like, and his only
request was for wisdom. The Lord replied: "It pleased the
Lord that Solomon had asked this. God said to him,
'Because you have asked this, and have not asked for

yourself long life or riches, or for the life of your enemies, but have asked for yourself understanding to discern what is right, I now do according to your word. Indeed I give you a wise and discerning mind; no one like you has been before you and no one like you shall arise after you. I give you also what you have not asked, both riches and honor all your life; no other king shall compare with you'" (1 Kings 3:10–13).

Daddy lived in a little, rundown house in a sketchy neighborhood and drove an old car. Since he could not afford a sofa, he had metal chairs in his otherwise empty living room. But his fortunes were elsewhere: "Store up for yourselves treasures in heaven, where neither moth nor rust consumes and where thieves do not break in and steal. For where your treasure is, there your heart will be also" (Matt 6:20–21). Daddy is with Jesus now, living in a fine mansion in his beautiful garden in heaven.

Years before that night in Waco, God had a divine plan to fulfill Daddy's wish through the book *Tell Everyone About Jesus* that I would write decades later. And before I ever prayed the Saint Francis prayer, God planned for Daddy to teach me how to truly forgive someone, and show me the blessings and miracles it can bring. As I wrote this book, Part II: "A Memoir of Forgiveness" came from Daddy's loving spirit. May the Holy Spirit touch all who read this book as it touched me.

> And he said to them, "Go into all the world and proclaim the good news to the whole creation."
> —Mark 16:15

Scripture Reference List

The following is a collection of significant scriptures used in the book for readers who wish to remember them for their spiritual growth.

1 Introduction

> Your word is a lamp to my feet and a light to my path.
> —Ps 119:105

> Let all be fully convinced in their own minds.
> —Rom 14:5b

3 Truth

> Ask, and it will be given you; search, and you will find; knock, and the door will be opened for you. For everyone who asks receives, and everyone who searches finds, and for everyone who knocks, the door will be opened.
> —Luke 11:9–10

> Love the Lord your God with all your heart, and with all your soul, and with all your mind.
> —Matt 22:37

> If any of you is lacking in wisdom, ask God, who gives to all generously and ungrudgingly, and it will be given you.
> —Jas 1:5

You will know the truth, and the truth will make
you free.
—John 8:32

4 SPIRITUALITY

The LORD God formed man of the dust of the
ground, and breathed into his nostrils the breath
of life; and man became a living soul.
—Gen 2:7 KJV

When God fashioned human beings, he planted
in them emotions and inclinations, but at the
same time he enthroned the mind among the
senses as a sacred governor over them all.
—4 Macc 2:21–22

My soul yearns for you in the night, my spirit
within me earnestly seeks you.
—Isa 26:9a

The human spirit is the lamp of the LORD,
searching every inmost part.
—Prov 20:27

For surely I know the plans I have for you, says
the LORD, plans for your welfare and not for
harm, to give you a future with hope. Then when
you call upon me and come and pray to me, I
will hear you. When you search for me, you will
find me; if you seek me with all your heart.
—Jer 29:11–13

5 BELIEFS & FAITH

All things can be done for the one who believes.
—Mark 9:23b

Faith is the assurance of things hoped for, the conviction of things not seen.
—Heb 11:1

He touched their eyes and said, "According to your faith let it be done to you." And their eyes were opened.
—Matt 9:29–30a

Whatever you ask for in prayer, believe that you have received it, and it will be yours.
—Mark 11:24

Do not worry about tomorrow, for tomorrow will bring worries of its own.
—Matt 6:34

6 WAS JESUS ON THE BUS?

One God and Father of all, who is above all and through all and in all.
—Eph 4:6

The God of peace, who brought back from the dead our Lord Jesus, the great shepherd of the sheep, by the blood of the eternal covenant.
—Heb 13:20

Before each person are life and death, and
whichever one chooses will be given.
—Sir 15:17

7 WHERE IS GOD?

As long as my breath is in me, and the spirit of
God is in my nostrils.
—Job 27:3

God did not send the Son into the world to
condemn the world, but in order that the world
might be saved through him.
—John 3:17

I am the way, and the truth, and the life. No one
comes to the Father except through me.
—John 14:6

Come to me, all you that are weary and are
carrying heavy burdens, and I will give you rest.
Take my yoke upon you, and learn from me; for I
am gentle and humble in heart, and you will find
rest for your souls. For my yoke is easy, and my
burden is light.
—Matt 11:28–30

It is not the children of the flesh who are the
children of God, but the children of the promise
are counted as descendants.
—Rom 9:8

For all who are led by the Spirit of God are children of God. For you did not receive a spirit of slavery to fall back into fear, but you have received a spirit of adoption.
—Rom 8:14–15b

8 THE IMAGE OF GOD

God created humankind in his image, in the image of God he created them; male and female he created them.
—Gen 1:27

The LORD, your God, is in your midst.
—Zeph 3:17a

God said to Moses, "I AM WHO I AM."
—Exod 3:14a

9 ON EARTH AS IT IS IN HEAVEN

The LORD your God is indeed God in heaven above and on earth below.
—Josh 2:11b

God made the two great lights—the greater light to rule the day and the lesser light to rule the night.
—Gen 1:16

The LORD God planted a garden in Eden, in the east; and there he put the man whom he had formed.
—Gen 2:8

A river flows out of Eden to water the garden, and from there it divides and becomes four branches.
—Gen 2:10

The kingdom of God cometh not with observation: Neither shall they say, Lo here! or, lo there! for, behold, the kingdom of God is within you.
—Luke 17:20–21 KJV

The LORD God took the man and put him in the garden of Eden to till it and keep it.
—Gen 2:15

Keep your heart with all vigilance, for from it flow the springs of life.
—Prov 4:23

God is love.
—1 John 4:16b

11 THE EGO NATURE

For what the flesh desires is opposed to the
Spirit, and what the Spirit desires is opposed to
the flesh.
—Gal 5:17

The serpent tricked me, and I ate.
—Gen 3:13b

12 A BIBLICAL TRAIL OF TWO NATURES

No one can serve two masters. Either you will
hate the one and love the other, or you will be
devoted to the one and despise the other.
—Matt 6:24a NIV

I am the good shepherd.
—John 10:14a

For the Son of Man came to seek out and to save
the lost.
—Luke 19:10

13 ABOUT JESUS

And the Word became flesh and lived among us.
—John 1:14a

He is the image of the invisible God, the
firstborn of all creation.
—Col 1:15

For in him the whole fullness of deity dwells
bodily.
—Col 2:9

For as all die in Adam, so all will be made alive
in Christ.
—1 Cor 15:22

In the beginning was the Word, and the Word
was with God, and the Word was God. He was in
the beginning with God. All things came into
being through him, and without him not one
thing came into being. What has come into being
in him was life, and the life was the light of all
people.
—John 1:1–4

It was he who created humankind in the
beginning, and he left them in the power of their
own free choice.
—Sir 15:14

Very truly, I tell you, no one can see the kingdom
of God without being born from above.
—John 3:3

What is born of the flesh is flesh, and what is
born of the Spirit is spirit. Do not be astonished
that I said to you, you must be born from above.
—John 3:6–7

The wind blows where it chooses, and you hear the sound of it, but you do not know where it comes from or where it goes. So it is with everyone who is born of the Spirit.
—John 3:8

Those who are unspiritual do not receive the gifts of God's Spirit, for they are foolishness to them, and they are unable to understand them because they are spiritually discerned.
—1 Cor 2:14

Look! He is coming with the clouds; every eye will see him, even those who pierced him.
—Rev 1:7

He was in the world, and the world came into being through him; yet the world did not know him.
—John 1:10

15 A ROSE FOR DADDY

Husbands should love their wives as they do their own bodies. He who loves his wife loves himself.
—Eph 5:28

16 OUR WACO VISIT

> If anyone is in Christ, there is a new creation:
> everything old has passed away; see, everything
> has become new!
> —2 Cor 5:17

> You do not even know what tomorrow will bring.
> —Jas 4:14a

> Jesus said, "Take away the stone."
> —John 11:39a

> Anyone who hears my word and believes him
> who sent me has eternal life, and does not come
> under judgment, but has passed from death to
> life.
> —John 5:24

> The one who rejects me and does not receive my
> word has a judge; on the last day the word that I
> have spoken will serve as judge.
> —John 12:48

> No testing has overtaken you that is not
> common to everyone. God is faithful, and he will
> not let you be tested beyond your strength, but
> with the testing he will also provide the way out
> so that you may be able to endure it.
> —1 Cor 10:13

Everyone therefore who acknowledges me before others, I also will acknowledge before my Father in heaven; but whoever denies me before others, I also will deny before my Father in heaven.
—Matt 10:32–33

Sleeper, awake! Rise from the dead, and Christ will shine on you.
—Eph 5:14

Your boasting is not a good thing. Do you not know that a little yeast leavens the whole batch of dough? Clean out the old yeast so that you may be a new batch, as you really are unleavened.
—1 Cor 5:6–7a

Those who drink of the water that I will give them will never be thirsty. The water that I will give will become in them a spring of water gushing up to eternal life.
—John 4:14

A new heart I will give you, and a new spirit I will put within you; and I will remove from your body the heart of stone and give you a heart of flesh.
—Ezek 36:26

God is spirit, and those who worship him must worship in spirit and truth.
—John 4:24

17 FRONT PORCH STORIES

> Where two or three are gathered in my name, I
> am there among them.
> —Matt 18:20

18 THE PRAYER OF SAINT FRANCIS OF ASSISI

> The Advocate, the Holy Spirit, whom the Father
> will send in my name, will teach you everything,
> and remind you of all that I have said to you.
> —John 14:26

19 FORTY YEARS EARLIER

> Make me to know your ways, O LORD;
> teach me your paths.
> —Ps 25:4

20 FIRST HOLY COMMUNION DAY

> He took a loaf of bread, and when he had given
> thanks, he broke it and gave it to them, saying,
> "This is my body, which is given for you. Do this
> in remembrance of me."
> —Luke 22:19

21 THE GRAVEYARD TOUR

> What is your life? For you are a mist that
> appears for a little while and then vanishes.
> —Jas 4:14b

22 SIXTEEN ROSARIES

> Trust in the LORD with all your heart, and do not rely on your own insight.
> —Prov 3:5

23 BACK TO THE PRAYER OF SAINT FRANCIS

> I love the LORD, because he has heard my voice and my supplications. Because he inclined his ear to me, therefore I will call on him as long as I live.
> —Ps 116:1–2

24 MEMORIES

> I thank my God every time I remember you.
> —Phil 1:3

25 THE EYES OF JESUS

> For "In him we live and move and have our being"; as even some of your own poets have said,
> "For we too are his offspring."
> —Acts 17:28

26 ABOUT THE THORNS

> We know that all things work together for good for those who love God, who are called according to his purpose.
> —Rom 8:28

27 FORGIVENESS

Be kind to one another, tenderhearted, forgiving one another, as God in Christ has forgiven you.
—Eph 4:32

Our purpose is to please God, not people. He alone examines the motives of our hearts.
—1 Thess 2:4 NLT

28 THE BEGGAR'S WISH

What is impossible for mortals is possible for God.
—Luke 18:27

Store up for yourselves treasures in heaven, where neither moth nor rust consumes and where thieves do not break in and steal. For where your treasure is, there your heart will be also.
—Matt 6:20–21

And he said to them, "Go into all the world and proclaim the good news to the whole creation."
—Mark 16:15

BIBLIOGRAPHY

Blacker, Carmen. "The Folklore of the Stranger: A Consideration of a Disguised Wandering Saint." Folklore vol 101:2, 162–168, 1990.
DOI: 10.1080/0015587X.1990.9715790

Cousins, Norman, and Rene Dubos. *Anatomy of an Illness as Perceived by the Patient: Reflections on Healing and Regeneration*. Boston, MA, USA: G. K. Hall, 1981.

Dyer, Wayne W. *The Power of Intention: Learning to Co-Create Your World Your Way*. Carlsbad, CA, USA: Hay House, 2004, 173.

Gide, Andre.' *Ainsi soit-il; ou, Les Jeux sont faits*. Paris, France: Gallimard, 1952, 174.

Goddard, Neville. "Neville Goddard Radio Lectures." Accessed January 1, 2022. https://realneville.com/txt/radio_lectures.htm.

Jammer, Max. *Einstein and Religion: Physics and Theology*. Princeton, NJ, USA: Princeton University Press, 1999, 93.

Shaw, George Bernard. *The Adventures of the Black Girl in Her Search for God*. Binghamton, NY, USA: Vail-Ballou Press, 1933, 53.

Wilson, Ian. *The Shroud of Turin: The Burial Cloth of Jesus Christ?* Garden City, NY, USA: Doubleday and Company, 1978.

Made in the USA
Columbia, SC
20 October 2023

24340093R00129